Kevin Pratt started his career as a writer on insurance topics with leading specialist trade publications. He is now a full-time freelance journalist writing for a variety of newspapers and magazines, including *The Sunday Times*, *The Times*, *The Daily Telegraph* and the *Financial Times*. He is a past winner of an annual journalists' award made by the British Insurance & Investment Brokers Association.

Also available in this series:

The Sunday Times Personal Finance Guide to Your Pension
STEPHEN ELLIS

The Sunday Times Personal Finance Guide to Your Home
DIANA WRIGHT

The Sunday Times Personal Finance Guide to Your Retirement
DIANA WRIGHT

The Sunday Times Personal Finance Guide to Tax-free Savings
CHRISTOPHER GILCHRIST

THE SUNDAY TIMES
Personal Finance Guide to

THE
PROTECTION
GAME

A Straightforward Guide to Insurance

Kevin Pratt

HarperCollins*Publishers*

HarperCollins*Publishers*,
77–85 Fulham Palace Road,
Hammersmith, London W6 8JB

A Paperback Original 1996
1 3 5 7 9 8 6 4 2

A catalogue record for this book
is available from the British Library

ISBN 0 00 638702 0

Set in Linotron Times by
Rowland Phototypesetting Limited,
Bury St Edmunds, Suffolk

Printed in Great Britain by
Caledonian International Book Manufacturer, Glasgow

CONTENTS

INTRODUCTION

Every year Britons spend an astonishing £25 billion on insuring their lives, their cars, their houses and belongings, and their health and well-being. That's more than the Gross National Product of most countries and accounts for the fact that insurance is one of the mainstays of the UK economy.

The typical UK family spends over £900 a year on insurance premiums of one sort or another – and that excludes any contributions made towards a pension. But how do any of us know for sure that we are getting the best out of our money? Are we buying the right sort of cover at the right price? Could we get a better deal? The answer is almost certainly 'yes'. There are few of us who would not benefit from a tip-to-toe examination of our insurance arrangements. This would help to identify the policies we do not really need and pinpoint the gaps in our cover.

This book is intended to aid this examination process. In clear language, it explains the jargon and technical waffle that surrounds so many insurance contracts. It is designed to enable you to find your way through the insurance maze and to give you ideas on improving your situation.

Protect and Survive

The desire to protect ourselves and our families and to provide for their well-being is a basic part of being human. In the past we might have had to battle the elements and guard against all manner of enemies, dangers and threats; these days it is financial security that is all important.

The dividing line between enjoying a comfortable lifestyle and

Table 1: Average yearly household expenditure on insurance

Home buildings	Home contents	Motor	Medical	Mortgage protection	Life	Other
£115.02	£87.05	£210.60	£35.36	£22.20	£426.56	£216.11

Source: Association of British Insurers

struggling to make ends meet can be perilously thin: even our sophisticated modern world can spring a multitude of nasty surprises. So it is very important to buy the right insurance policies and create an effective safety net under yourself and your loved ones: if the unexpected happens, you can then limit the effects and cope with the consequences.

Choice of policies
It is the proud boast of the insurance industry that anything and everything can be insured: space rockets, footballers' legs, oil rigs and pop singers' vocal chords have all been covered. There is certainly a wide range of contracts designed for the needs of normal individuals and families. You can insure against death, illness or accident; you can protect your car and your house; you can use insurance to help provide care when you get old or to meet your bills should you be unable to earn a living; you can even insure your pets against the cost of vet's bills.

With such a bewildering array of insurance contracts from which to choose, it is worth knowing a little bit about the way the insurance business is structured. This will help you decide where to go to obtain the right policy at the right price.

How insurance is sold
Insurance is sold in many different ways by many different organizations. Every day you will be bombarded with advertisements offering you all sorts of policies. How do you know which company to buy from?

An increasing number of insurance companies are selling their wares direct to the public through television and newspaper advertisements. These firms usually provide a telephone number that allows you to obtain a quote and arrange cover immediately. In addition to these 'direct sellers' there are various brokers, consultants, advisers and agents who sell insurance on behalf of someone else. Most banks and building societies, for instance, act as insurance sales outlets. They can arrange various types of cover and often include details of the products they offer when they send out their account statements. Some of the big high street organizations even have their own insurance companies and offer their products in the branches.

Smaller, local organizations sell insurance on behalf of a large number of insurance companies. They may specialize in insurance for cars and houses, or in investment plans; or they may offer advice on insurance and investment matters. You may also find yourself being offered insurance by companies that have no obvious connection with the business. If you buy a new car, for example, you may receive a year's free motor insurance cover from the manufacturer or through the dealership. Department stores are also branching out into the insurance world. There is certainly no shortage of choice.

Choosing where to buy
Not all insurance brokers and advisers are the same. They fall into two main camps:

- **'Independent' advisers**, whose job is to hunt among a wide range of insurance companies for the most appropriate and best-value policy
- **Agents**, who only sell on behalf of one insurance company.

You may encounter both these types when arranging insurance on your house, for example. If you have a mortgage, your building society will probably offer a buildings insurance policy produced in conjunction with an insurance company. But you could also consult an independent broker in order to obtain quotations from a range of other insurance companies.

Whichever type of salesperson you buy your insurance from, part of your premium will be used to pay the salesperson's commission. This normally accounts for around 15% of the price you pay, although banks and building societies have been able to negotiate much higher commissions of up to 30%. This is because they can promise the insurance companies a steady flow of business from their mortgage customers.

Of course, those insurance companies that sell direct do not have to pay commission to middlemen – something they often mention in their advertisements. However, there is no guarantee that the direct route will always be the cheapest. The direct seller still has its wages bill to meet and it has to buy a large amount of advertising space in order to attract your attention in the first place. And if you think the freephone number is a good idea, remember who is paying for it with their premiums!

What does a middleman do?
When you pay commission to a middleman, what do you get for your money? The job of an independent adviser – someone who sells on behalf of more than one insurance company – is to act in your best interests. In other words, the independent adviser is *your* agent, rather than the agent of the insurance company. This means that the adviser is there to fight your corner if, for example, you ever have to make a claim. This can be more than a psychological comfort; having someone on your side when dealing with the insurance company can be of great practical benefit. After all, the broker will be able to explain the technicalities of the issue and put your side of the argument in terms the insurance company will understand.

If you buy direct from the insurance company, you are on your own when it comes to dealing with them. Of course, this need not be a problem. Direct companies often pride themselves on offering a friendly and efficient service. However, you may still decide that it is worth paying your commission in order to have someone working for you who knows the ins and outs of the insurance business.

Paying by instalment

Most people pay for their annual insurance policies (such as household and motor cover) in one go each year, but increasingly, insurers are accepting payments by instalment. Premiums often amount to several hundred pounds, or even over £1,000, so it can be a great help to spread the cost over the year.

A few insurers levy a charge if you want to pay monthly (you might, for example, find the premium increased by 5%). However, it is more and more common for the gross premium simply to be divided by 12 in order to arrive at the monthly figure. You may even obtain a small discount if you set up a standing order or direct debit in favour of the insurance company.

Insurance companies like instalments because, once the customer gets into the routine of paying every month, they are more likely to renew that policy rather than hunting around for an alternative.

Insurance Premium Tax

In the 1993 Budget the Government announced its intention to introduce a brand-new form of taxation, to be known as Insurance Premium Tax, or IPT. It was actually first levied in October 1994 and is now charged on virtually every form of insurance that is renewed annually, including motor, household, private medical cover and other protection policies. It is not charged, however, on life insurance policies or contracts that contain an investment element.

IPT is currently set at 2.5% of the gross premium, which means that for every £100 you pay to the insurer, you have to pay £2.50 to the Treasury. Most insurers will quote the actual amount of IPT on your policy details. Although IPT is a relatively new tax in the UK, it is quite commonplace elsewhere in Europe – often at much higher rates. For example, in France the equivalent of IPT for fire insurance is 30%!

Complaints about your insurance

If things do go wrong or you feel you have not been treated fairly over your insurance, you have a number of avenues open to you. Every company will have its own complaints procedure, so it is worth writing to the chairman or chief executive of the organization concerned. If this fails, you might consider taking your case to one of the various ombudsmen connected with the insurance industry. It is their job to adjudicate over disputes and to decide what further action, if any, should be taken. Insurance companies and brokers often belong to trade associations and writing to these can often help in some instances. A list of useful addresses appears in Chapter 11 (see page 135).

1 ‖ *Life Insurance*

Life insurance, or life *assurance*, as it is sometimes known, comes in many different forms. At its simplest, it should perhaps be called 'death insurance', since the policy only pays out when the insured person dies. This is what might be called a pure protection contract, as opposed to a policy that combines protection with an investment plan.

Some insurance policies include a high investment element and provide little actual insurance protection. These are variously known as 'single premium bonds', 'guaranteed equity bonds' or 'guaranteed income plans' and they are largely beyond the scope of this book. However, technically these are insurance products and are certainly offered by insurance companies and their representatives. If you are primarily interested in protecting yourself and the financial well-being of your family in the event of your death, you should consider very carefully whether these investment-oriented plans are your best bet. If you are interested in an investment product, the first port of call should be an independent financial adviser (IFA). You can get a list of IFAs in your area by contacting IFA Promotion (see page 139).

As far as protection policies are concerned, a number of names have evolved for the various contracts that are available.

Term Insurance

Term insurance provides protection for a given period of time – known as the 'term'. You are not investing money, and if you live until the end of the term, you kiss goodbye to your premiums and get nothing in return. If, for any reason, you stop paying premiums during the term, you are no longer protected and the policy will not pay out if you die. This is what the insurance companies mean when they say that the policy has 'lapsed'.

When you buy term insurance, you select a 'sum assured' – this is the amount that will be paid out in the event of death during the term. When deciding on this figure, you need to think about what you want the money to do. Do you have any outstanding debts that would need to be settled? If you have a family that relies on you, how much would they need if you were no longer in a position to provide for them?

If you have a partner – and especially if you have children – it is important that both of you have term cover protection, even if only one of you is earning. Think what would happen if the partner looking after the house and the children died. The surviving partner would have to continue working in order to maintain the family income, but how would the extra help needed at home be paid for?

Many companies offer protection on a 'joint life, first death' basis. This means that both partners are insured under the same policy and that the policy will pay out if and when the first one dies within the term. The survivor will then have the sum assured to help him or her through the ensuing financial headaches.

How much cover should I have?
To gain an idea of how much insurance protection you should have, it is worth noting down your family's income and expenditure and thinking how these figures would be affected by your death or that of your partner.

- What is your gross income from all sources? Remember any regular overtime, commissions or bonuses and income from savings and investments, such as building society interest and share dividends.
- How much of your income do you spend? In other words,

how much does it cost to maintain the family home? Write down all your financial commitments and calculate what it would cost to maintain the home and look after the children if the partner who is primarily responsible for these tasks were to die.

- How much do you owe? If you die, those to whom you owe money might demand immediate repayment from your estate. In addition to the mortgage, remember credit card bills and anything you have bought on hire purchase.
- Do you or does your partner have a company car? If so, what would you use if you no longer had it? How much would it cost to replace?
- What about the future? How old are your children? If you were to die, for how many years would your partner need financial help to look after them? Remember the cost of schooling and further education. And think also of elderly relatives: you may already be helping them financially, so you should consider how your death might affect a loved one's well-being in the future.

Insurance advisers often reckon that a person's sum insured should relate to their annual earnings. Again, there is no precise figure, but it might be reasonable to suggest that a person should be insured for ten times their annual income. This may seem like an awful lot, but it is better to have too much protection than too little. There is a limit on how big the sum insured should be, however, since the size of the premium is partly determined by the size of the sum insured. Clearly, you do not want to waste money by buying insurance protection that you don't need.

It is also worth taking into account any life insurance you may already have. For instance, if you belong to a company pension scheme, it may provide a 'death in service' benefit. This is a lump sum payment made to your chosen beneficiary if you die and is often fixed at three or four times your annual earnings. If you belong to a pension scheme, have your own personal pension or are self-employed, you can obtain tax relief on your term insurance premiums if you organize the policy through your pension policy. Premiums will not qualify for tax relief otherwise.

A number of other factors affect the size of the premium. Here are some of the questions you will be asked:

- Date of birth.
- Sex.
- Are you a smoker?
- How much cover do you need?
- For how long do you require cover?
- Do you want cover just for yourself or for you and a partner?
- Do you have dependants?
- Do you have a company pension scheme or a personal pension?
- Are you self-employed?
- Is the policy designed to cover a specific liability, such as a mortgage?

Naturally, older people and those in poor health will pay more as they are more likely to die during the term, and so the insurance company is more likely to have to pay out. The same is true of smokers. Those in dangerous occupations, such as steeplejacks, miners, oil-rig workers and so on, will face higher premiums because of the risks associated with their work. Men often have to pay more because their life expectancy is not as good as that of women.

In some instances – when the sum insured is very high, for example – the insurance company will ask you to undergo a medical examination before deciding whether to offer cover and how high the premium rate should be. Alternatively, they may write to your GP to confirm your medical history. If a medical is required, it will be arranged at a time to suit you and paid for by the insurance company.

The length of the term will also affect the premium. Clearly, there is more chance of someone dying over the course of, say, the next 20 years than over the next 10.

Table 2: Sample monthly term assurance premiums

Age at next birthday	Length of term	Sum assured		
		£200,000	*£500,000*	*£1,000,000*
30	5 years	£14.40	£33.00	£64.00
30	10 years	£18.00	£42.00	£82.00
40	5 years	£23.40	£55.50	£109.00
40	10 years	£36.40	£88.00	£174.00

Source: Commercial Union

Where to buy your policy

It is always worth shopping around when you want term insurance. This is one of the few insurance contracts where you can choose the company on the basis of price alone, so value for money is easy to identify – and the savings can be significant. For example, a couple taking out insurance to cover their £60,000 mortgage would pay £3,000 more in premiums if they picked the tenth-cheapest company rather than the cheapest.

If you go to an independent adviser, he or she will do the shopping around on your behalf.

Trusts

When you arrange term insurance protection, you should be offered the opportunity to have the policy written 'under trust'. This means that the proceeds of the policy can be paid directly to the person you nominate – the beneficiary – rather than be paid into your estate. This is important because money paid into your estate can be difficult to get at and your surviving partner will probably need funds straight away. Also, if the proceeds of a life insurance policy find their way into your estate, they may be liable to inheritance tax (IHT).

Variations on a theme

Even with an apparently straightforward insurance policy like term insurance, there are a number of variations. For example, some policies can be renewed at the end of the original term without any requirement to produce further evidence of good health. This 'renewable' type of term cover provides older people with a better deal than they would get if they were starting from scratch. The premiums will still rise on renewal, however, to take account of their more advanced age.

It is also possible to 'convert' term insurance policies in order to extend the scope of the protection. For example, you might convert your term policy into an endowment, which offers an investment element in addition to basic insurance protection. This conversion can be made without the need to provide further evidence of health, which is obviously good news for those whose health has declined during the period.

However, you do have to pay more for the conversion option, so this sort of policy may not be worth the extra cost. If you decide you want a savings plan, you might be better off choosing a dedicated investment product, such as a personal equity plan (Pep), rather than adapting a protection contract. It would certainly not make good sense to feel obliged to convert your term assurance plan rather than pick another sort of investment simply because you wanted to take advantage of your option.

You should also bear in mind that the skills required to run a term assurance policy are very different from those required to manage an investment policy. Insurance companies may do both, but some term assurance specialists have less than sparkling investment records. When you come to consider investment options, you may decide against converting because your company is not among the better performers.

Decreasing term insurance

Straightforward term insurance has a fixed sum assured and a premium that remains level throughout the life of the policy. With decreasing term insurance the sum assured gradually goes down over the course of the term (although the premiums usually remain constant). This sort of policy is often used to cover a debt that is gradually being repaid. If term insurance is being used by someone with a repayment (or 'capital and interest') mortgage, it will probably be called a mortgage protection policy.

Decreasing term cover can also be used to protect against a *potential* liability – for example, when planning for possible inheritance tax (IHT) charges. The IHT rules state that large financial gifts made within seven years of the giver's death will be taxed on a sliding scale. A seven-year decreasing term policy can therefore be arranged to meet any tax charge that might arise.

Term cover and mortgages
As already mentioned, term assurance only ever pays out if the policyholder dies. This means it can only ever repay a mortgage in the event of a death. If the borrower survives to the end of the term, the policy has no value.

If your mortgage is an interest-only loan rather than a straightforward repayment deal, you will need a separate repayment plan, such as an endowment policy, a pension or a series of Peps. Some of these come with life insurance built in, but others are pure investment contracts. If this is the case, you will need to arrange additional term cover to repay the debt if you die before the investment has grown to the required amount.

If two of you are contributing to the cost of a mortgage but the investment contract and the attached life insurance are in the name of one or the other, it is necessary to arrange separate term

Table 3: Inheritance tax – reduced charges on lifetime gifts within 7 years of death

Years between gift and death	Percentage of death rates applicable
0–3	100%
3–4	80%
4–5	60%
5–6	40%
6–7	20%

insurance so that both of you are insured. If this is not done, the surviving partner might suddenly be faced with having to meet the monthly commitments on one income.

Family income benefit

Decreasing term insurance is also marketed under the name 'Family Income Benefit'. You buy this type of cover to provide for those left behind after the death of the family breadwinner. Instead of paying out a lump sum like a normal term insurance contract, these policies pay out a monthly income from the time of the policyholder's death to the end of the original term. If you were to die 15 years into a 20-year term, for example, payments would be made to your beneficiaries for the remaining five years.

It is also possible to arrange *increasing* term insurance. This type of policy allows you to counter the effects of inflation by increasing the sum assured during the term. You might also opt for the increasing option if your earnings are rising as your career develops – you will want more cover to replace your family's increasing spending power.

If you increase the sum assured, you will be charged higher premiums to reflect your advancing age, but no fresh evidence of good health will be necessary, which will make it cheaper than taking out a new policy from scratch.

Whole of Life Insurance

Term insurance, as we have seen, protects you for a certain length of time. Whole of life cover, as the name suggests, protects you for the whole of your life. This means that, whenever you die, the policy will pay out the benefit.

Whole of life insurance is more expensive than term insurance because, sooner or later, a claim will inevitably be made; with term insurance, a proportion of policyholders survive to the end of their term. The actual cost of whole of life cover, however, is determined by the same age and health considerations that apply to term insurance. Insurance companies calculate whole of life premium payments so that they need only be made up to a certain age, such as 65 or 75. This allows for the fact that older people may not be in a position to maintain the payments.

Term insurance remains the best bet for those who want to make sure that they do not leave any nasty debts behind them and that their families will not be plunged into financial crisis after their death. Whole of life cover, by contrast, is suitable for those who want to build up an investment legacy that they can pass on after their death.

Investment elements
When you buy whole of life protection, you have a choice: you can either select a fixed sum assured or you can choose a policy where the size of the eventual pay-out depends on investment growth. These investment policies also have a sum assured: this is the minimum amount the policy will pay in the event of death. The sum assured will be set at quite a low figure, the intention being to add funds on top to produce a bigger amount for when the claim is made.

If the first route is taken, you have to consider the impact of inflation over the years. What sounds like a huge amount of money in today's terms may seem insubstantial when the claim is made. The second route is devised to help you get round this problem by boosting the sum assured over the years.

If the insurance company is successful and produces good investment performance, the policy should keep pace with the rising cost of living. However, insurance companies will not guarantee a certain level of investment performance, so it is vital to choose the right company. It may well be worth taking independent advice to help you decide which companies offer the best prospects.

Two investment methods are used with whole of life policies: 'with profits' and 'unit-linked'. As is often the case with insurance matters, the language used can be confusing and intimidating, so it is a good idea to look at what these phrases actually mean.

With profits

Insurance companies love their technical terms. The phrase 'with profits' may seem off-putting, but it is a reasonably accurate description of how certain policies work. It simply means that the policyholder shares in any profits made by the insurance company (once deductions have been made for its management expenses and other costs, such as shareholder dividends). Profits come as a result of the company's success in investing in the Stock Market, commercial property and financial securities such as bonds and Government-issued 'gilts'.

These profits are distributed to policyholders in the form of 'bonuses', of which there are two types. 'Reversionary' (sometimes known as 'annual' or 'interim') bonuses are paid every year, while 'terminal' bonuses are paid when a policy matures or a claim is payable.

'Reversionary' is another of those odd words. It actually means that, although the bonuses are awarded each year throughout the life of the policy, the policyholder or the beneficiaries cannot get their hands on them until the benefits 'revert' to the policyholder. With a whole of life policy, this is when a claim is made. With other sorts of investment contract, this is when the policy 'matures' at the end of a specified length of time. Once a reversionary bonus is awarded, it cannot subsequently be taken away again.

To complicate the issue further, reversionary bonuses come in two forms depending on the type of policy and the insurance company concerned. A 'simple' reversionary bonus is a percentage of the original sum assured (which, remember, is the minimum amount that the policy will pay out if a claim is made). A 'compound' reversionary bonus, by contrast, is a percentage both of the sum assured and past bonuses that have already been awarded. The total amount of bonus grows much more quickly with this compounding effect.

Table 4: Simple and reversionary bonuses – a comparison

Sum assured: £10,000

End of year	Simple bonus of 5%	Sum assured
1	£500	£10,500
2	£500	£11,000
3	£500	£11,500
4	£500	£12,000
5	£500	£12,500
6	£500	£13,000
7	£500	£13,500
8	£500	£14,000
9	£500	£14,500
10	£500	£15,000

End of year	Compound bonus of 5%	Sum assured
1	£500	£10,500
2	£525	£11,025
3	£551	£11,576
4	£579	£12,155
5	£608	£12,763
6	£638	£13,400
7	£670	£14,070
8	£703	£14,774
9	£739	£15,513
10	£776	£16,289

Insurance companies vary widely in their attitude to bonuses. Some pay higher reversionary bonuses and lower terminal bonuses: this means that those who claim in years when profits are poor and terminal bonuses are low do not suffer unduly. Others pay lower reversionary bonuses so that they can hold money in reserve and thus maintain higher terminal bonuses, even when their profits in a particular year are disappointing.

Choosing between different with-profits policies is a matter of individual judgement, so you may well need independent financial advise when choosing the right insurance company for your particular circumstances.

Unit-linked insurance

This is a phrase that means little to anyone without an insurance background, but again the idea is relatively simple. Each premium you pay buys units in an investment fund (in which there may be many thousands of other 'unit-holders' like you). This fund is invested by the insurance company in stocks and shares, the commercial property market or other financial instruments, and the value of your units is linked directly to the investment performance. It will therefore fluctuate in value but obviously it should increase over time if the insurance company is any good. When a claim is made or the policy matures, the units are cashed in and you or your beneficiaries receive the proceeds.

This unit-linked approach allows you to keep a close track of how the value of your policy is moving. You will also have a wide selection of investment funds from which to choose, which means you can control, to a degree, how your premiums are invested. If you have a with profits contract, you do not have the same opportunity to influence the management of your money.

Endowments

Term insurance and whole of life policies are primarily protection contracts; an endowment is an investment policy with an element of protection built in. With profits and unit-linked versions are available.

Endowments run for a certain number of years, usually 10, 15, 20 or 25. At the end of this period the policy is said to 'mature'. At this point the basic sum assured (which is fixed at the outset) and any accumulated investment returns are paid out. If the policy-holder dies before the end of the term, the sum assured and any accumulated returns made up to that point are paid out.

Endowment policies became very popular in the 1970s and 1980s as a means of paying off an interest-only mortgage; they are still sold for this purpose, although with profits contracts in particular have attracted criticism of late because of their inflexibility. There has also been concern that 'low cost' endowments might not generate sufficient returns to pay off the outstanding loan at maturity. Low cost endowments, the most widely sold form of endowment, are explained in detail later (see page 21).

With profits endowments really only work if they are allowed to run to their full term, when the terminal bonus is paid. This means that homebuyers have little opportunity to pay off their mortgage early if they want to. What is more, it is easy to see how problems might arise if a couple were to split up before the endowment matured – there is no way for the value of the policy to be divided until maturity, except by selling it, which, as you will see, is not always practical.

There can also be problems with unit-linked endowments because of fluctuations in the value of the fund in which the premiums are invested. Reversionary bonuses on with profits policies lock in a certain amount of growth because, once given, they cannot be taken away. With a unit-linked fund, however, you are always exposed to the danger of a sudden fall in the value of the fund. For this reason, many insurance companies recommend that policyholders switch to a less-volatile fund as the maturity date of their policy approaches. This is not a fool-proof method of securing the investment, however; risks always remain.

The worries that low cost endowments, both with profits and unit-linked, might not grow sufficiently to repay the policyholders' mortgages have stimulated interest in other repayment policies, such as personal equity plans (Peps). The basic problem is that, in the early and mid 1980s, insurance companies enjoyed a golden period of high profits, when maturing endowments were often worth considerably more than the mortgage they were designed to settle. This prompted some insurance companies and financial advisers to make increasingly optimistic predictions about the rates of investment growth that could be expected.

In October 1987, however, the investment boom came to an abrupt halt with the 'Black Monday' stock market crash. The lost ground has been recouped in the intervening years, but investment returns generally have declined and the impressive figures of a decade ago are no longer available. The over-optimism of the salesmen in the mid 1980s has been exposed.

Nowadays we even see instances where policyholders have been asked to increase their premiums in order to ensure that the endowment remains on course to settle the debt at the end of the term. Insurance companies review their mortgage-linked endowments at regular intervals and will let you know if things are going awry. This gives you the opportunity to put things right, but it does mean that you will have to find the extra money for the bigger premium.

All this has led to a general scaling-down of expectations from endowment policies. The regulators of the insurance industry have told insurance companies and financial advisers that projections of what a policy might be worth in the future must conform to strict, more realistic guidelines.

If you choose the right company and your endowment runs to its full term, the returns can be impressive. However, other investment products, such as unit trusts and investment trusts (especially when sheltered from tax within a Pep), might be more appropriate, depending on your requirements. Again, an independent adviser will be able to guide you through the various options.

Endowments and tax

Companies and advisers selling endowments make much of the fact that the proceeds from a maturing policy are 'tax-free'. While this is true in the sense that policyholders do not have to pay tax on the lump sum they receive, it is not strictly true to say that it has never been taxed. Insurance companies have to pay tax on the profts they make, so while they are investing your premiums, they are also paying tax on the money they are making on your behalf. It is more accurate to think of the proceeds of your policy as 'tax-paid'.

Endowment policies have to conform to certain rules in order to qualify for this 'tax-paid' status. One of these requires the policy to be maintained for a certain period (either 10 years or three-quarters of its term, whichever is shorter); otherwise higher-rate taxpayers may find themselves facing an extra tax charge on any proceeds they receive.

Low cost endowments

Far and away the most common form of endowment – the low cost version – is in fact a combination of an endowment and a decreasing term insurance policy. It was developed by insurance companies to take advantage of the booming market in mortgage repayment policies in the 1970s and 80s. If you already have an endowment with which you are planning to repay your mortgage, it is likely to be a low cost version.

Low cost endowments carry lower premiums than standard 'full' endowments because the basic sum assured is kept deliberately low; someone with a £40,000 mortgage, for example, might have a basic sum assured of only £15,000. If the policyholder were to die during the term of the endowment, the debt would be cleared by the cheaper decreasing term assurance; in this way, the outstanding debt is always covered.

The overall intention is to add bonuses to the sum assured so that it grows to match, and perhaps even out-grows, the actual mortgage.

Low start endowments

These policies offer lower premiums in the early years and make up the shortfall later on. They were introduced in recognition of the fact that many homebuyers, particularly those taking out a mortgage for the first time, often operate on tight budgets. However, they will probably be able to afford higher premiums as salaries rise and other financial commitments fall.

With these policies, the premiums are set at a deliberately low level in year one; then, over the course of the next five years, they increase in stages until they settle at a fixed level for the remainder of the life of the policy. Clearly, it is important for those taking out low start endowments to be prepared for the increasing premiums over the first five years.

Surrendering endowments and the alternatives

As noted earlier, with profits endowments have been criticized because of their inflexibility; they work well if they are maintained until they mature, but policyholders may receive a poor deal if, for whatever reason, they want to dissolve the arrangement early.

Life insurance companies offer a 'surrender value' to those endowment policyholders who wish to obtain a cash sum from their policy or who can no longer afford the premiums. Surrender values in the early years of the contract are notoriously low because the initial premiums are absorbed in the cost of setting up the policy (such as management expenses and commissions paid to sales staff and intermediaries); in some cases policholders may even get back a smaller sum than they have paid in.

Recent changes in the way life insurance companies operate mean that they have to tell potential policyholders what they might expect in terms of surrender values at different points throughout the term of the policy. This has stimulated competition and some surrender values have crept up. However, early surrender – nearly always results in the loss of the vital terminal bonus, so the overall value of the policy will always be disappointing.

Policyholders contemplating surrender, either because they cannot afford the premiums or because they need to get their hands on some cash, have two other options. They can apply to the insurance company for a policy loan; or they can 'sell' their policy to someone else, who agrees to continue paying the premiums in order to collect the maturity value (or receive the sum insured if the policyholder dies before the policy matures).

The loan route often appeals to those who are going through a lean patch and simply want to realize what cash they can from their policy. Insurance companies tend to charge rates of interest in line with those levied by banks on personal loans. The maximum loan advance is likely to be 90% of the surrender value and the underlying value of the policy will be used as security. If the policholder meets the interest payments, the policy will remain 'in force', which means a claim can still be made on it.

Policies can be sold either at auction or through one of the growing number of traders in 'second-hand' endowments. Buyers are often prepared to pay a higher price than the surrender value because of the potential investment return on a mature policy. Even when commissions and expenses are taken into account, the seller can see a handsome return. Dealers in second-hand endowments usually stipulate that the policy must have been running for a certain length of time, perhaps five years, and there will probably be a minimum surrender value – typically £1,500, but ultimately depending on the company concerned. Dealers also look for policies issued by established and reputable insurance companies. A large number of companies operate in the second-hand endowment market. A list of names appears in Appendix 1 (see page 139).

Some policyholders have been put off selling their life insurance policies because, even when the policy is sold, it is still their own life that is insured. The worry is that the new owner of the policy might be tempted to kill them in order to claim on the policy. However, this is not a realistic possibility because a large proportion of the value of a with profits endowment is contained in the terminal bonus. Far from welcoming the death of the life insured, the purchaser of a second-hand endowment is much more likely to celebrate that person's living until the policy matures.

As ever, it is essential to obtain expert and independent advice before deciding what to do in this sort of situation.

2 || *Household Insurance*

There are two main types of household insurance: buildings cover, and contents cover. It is possible to have both types of cover with the same insurance company under a 'combined' policy, or to arrange separate policies. If you are living in rented accommodation, you need only arrange contents cover.

Some insurance companies specialize in one sort of cover, so it is worth obtaining a number of quotes. Many companies will be only too happy to provide both sorts of cover, even though their rates for one of the contracts may not be particularly competitive: this is why it is such a good idea to shop around.

Household insurance, like motor insurance, is an extremely competitive market at the moment, with an increasing number of companies selling direct to the public in competition with established firms of brokers and agents. This is driving prices down, but it is probably still necessary to get quotes both from direct insurers and an independent adviser to be sure of getting a good deal.

It is certainly worth going into the market to check on prices if you have been with your existing insurer for a number of years. Many policyholders tend to renew their household covers automatically with the same firm year after year (unlike motor insurance, where people are more likely to shop around). Even if you decide to stay with the same firm, it is important to check the renewal documents every year: insurers sometimes change the terms of the policy, which means you may be disappointed when it comes to making a claim.

Buildings Cover

Insuring your house is basic common sense. What would you do if it were destroyed and there was no money to replace it? Of course, there is no law saying you have to have insurance, but it is hard to see why anyone would try to do without it. And if you have a mortgage, you will probably have no choice: mortgage lenders, not unreasonably, insist that the building against which they advance the mortgage must be insured for the amount that it would cost to rebuild it. Otherwise, if the house were destroyed, they would be left with no security for the outstanding loan.

Buildings insurance is essential, but at least you have plenty of choice when it comes to finding the best deal. Competition has been particularly ferocious in this area of the insurance market in recent years as insurance companies and brokers have tried to break the virtual monopoly of banks and building societies, which act both as mortgage lenders and insurance providers and are consequently in a position to persuade homebuyers to insure their house at the same time as they arrange their loan.

Many borrowers readily agree because they trust the organization and assume they are being offered an attractive policy. They may also think that, by refusing to buy the policy from the lender, they may jeopardize the mortgage deal itself. These fears are only partially justified. On fixed rate mortgage deals lenders are allowed to insist that borrowers take out insurance (sometimes for contents as well as buildings cover) as a part of the package. On traditional mortgages, where the rate of interest varies, lenders are not allowed to make the loan conditional on the purchase of insurance. However, they are allowed to charge an 'administration fee' (usually £25) if borrowers seek to make their own arrangements. This fee is ostensibly to cover the costs involved in checking that the cover is adequate, but there is little doubt that it is also levied to deter people from shopping around for a better deal.

In the vast majority of cases a better deal *would* be found elsewhere. This is because building societies in particular have negotiated huge commissions from their select panels of insurers – commissions that the insurers are happy to pay because of the volume of business involved. Now this situation is being challenged, both by companies that sell direct (and therefore do not pay commissions) and by companies that pay more modest commissions to other advisers.

Even when the £25 or even £50 administration fee is taken into account, the insurance can work out cheaper if you buy it elsewhere. And it should be remembered that savings will continue each year, while the fee is a one-off charge. Some insurance companies are discounting the first year's buildings premium by the equivalent of an administration fee in a bid to attract business. Details of these offers can be found by consulting a broker or by shopping around among the direct insurers.

The 'sum insured'

When you arrange buildings insurance you need to decide on the 'sum insured', which is the amount the insurance company would pay out if your home were to be completely destroyed by an insured 'peril'. This figure should be your best estimate of how much it would cost to rebuild the house; it is *not* the price the property would fetch if it were sold on the open market. This is an important distinction because one of the principal factors affecting the buildings insurance premium will be the size of the sum insured; in many cases the property is worth significantly more than it would cost to rebuild, so a policyholder could end up paying more than is necessary.

You can find out the correct rebuilding value from the survey undertaken when the property was bought. It is important that this valuation is reviewed regularly so that it takes into account increases in rebuilding costs. Most lenders link the rebuilding value to the House Rebuilding Cost Index, which is produced by the Royal Institution of Chartered Surveyors.

Where a survey does not exist, you might consider commissioning a new one. They usually cost in the region of £75 to £100.

Alternatively, you could take informal advice from neighbours living in similar properties. The insurance company or broker might also be able to give a suitable figure. Some companies will conduct surveys of their own, especially on properties worth £250,000 or more.

It is certainly worth making sure that the sum insured is realistic in order to avoid the imposition of the 'average' clause when a claim is made.

The 'average' clause
Insurers build the average clause into policies to protect themselves. Some policyholders deliberately choose an unrealistically low sum insured in order to reduce the premium, which means the insurer effectively carries more risk than is justified by the premium paid. The average clause allows the insurer to pay a proportion of the claim – a proportion determined by the difference between the chosen sum insured and the true rebuilding cost.

Let us suppose you insure your house for £50,000 and submit a claim for flood damage of £20,000. While investigating the claim, the insurance company realizes that the actual rebuilding cost is £100,000 or twice the chosen sum insured. The company then applies the average clause and only pays 50% of the claim – £10,000.

Calculating the cost of buildings insurance
When the sum insured is agreed, the insurer quotes a price, usually in terms of pence per hundred pounds; this is used to calculate the premium. For example, if the rate is 25p per £100, the policyholder will pay 25p for every £100 of the sum insured; a property with a £100,000 sum insured would therefore attract a premium of £250. Some insurers quote their rates in pounds per thousand, in which case this rate would appear as £2.50 per £1,000.

Buildings insurance rates are determined by the likelihood that the property will be damaged by flood, storm, falling trees, subsidence, landslip and heave. Various other risks are covered, such as fire and damage caused by vehicles or animals, but these are considered to be more or less an equal threat to every property. It is therefore the situation of the house and the prevailing weather conditions in the area that influence the rate.

When an insurance company is considering what price to charge for buildings insurance, it will consider the proximity of the property to the sea, to rivers and other bodies of water and will check whether the area has a history of flooding. General weather patterns will also be scrutinized to see whether the location is prone to violent storms. If the property is surrounded by trees, the rate might be increased to reflect the risk of one being brought down onto the house.

Subsidence

Subsidence and other earth movements have been a problem for insurers in recent years because of prolonged spells of drought in the 1970s and 80s. These weakened the foundations of many properties, particularly those built on clay soils to the north and south of London and elsewhere in the south and east of England. This means that the price you pay will be determined to a degree by where you live. Insurance companies use geological maps to find out whether your house is built on solid, reliable granite or insecure, risky clay. However, some maps are more precise than others. Many predominantly clay areas, for example, contain granite shelves that are unlikely to suffer any subsidence. If the insurance company's map does not recognize this, a house built on the granite may simply be lumped in with those built on clay and attract a high premium as a result – another good reason to shop around.

Further difficulties have arisen because many housing developments in recent decades have involved the planting of large numbers of trees close to the properties. As they grew, their roots sometimes damaged foundations or drew sufficient moisture from the soil to otherwise weaken the structure. It should be noted that a policy will not pay out if subsidence occurs because of the negligence or incompetence of the builder. If you buy a new home, you should receive a guarantee for at least 10 years against subsidence-related problems, which the builder will be obliged to put right.

Insurers are also likely to charge a higher premium on buildings situated near cliff-tops, since coastal erosion has claimed a number of properties in recent years. Areas where there is a history of mining may also be seen as higher risk, since the settlement of old workings could have an impact at the surface.

Insurance companies have responded to the increased incidence of subsidence by introducing stiff 'excesses' on subsidence claims. An excess – or 'deductible' – is the amount the policyholder is expected to contribute towards the cost of a claim. This may be set at £500 – or even as high as £5,000 in high-risk areas.

Further subsidence problems have arisen in the past when people have, for whatever reason, changed insurers. It was not unusual, when the subsidence was discovered, for the new insurer to deny liability on the basis that the problem started before it became responsible for the risk. The old insurer, meanwhile, would often argue that it was no longer involved with that particular property and was not interested in any claims arising out of it.

The insurers' trade body, the Association of British Insurers (ABI), sorted out this mess in 1994 by introducing the Domestic Subsidence Agreement. This lays down that claims made within eight weeks of a new policy being taken out should be accepted and dealt with by the previous insurer. If the claim is made one year or more after the current policy is taken out, the current insurer has to deal with and, if appropriate, settle the claim. During the intervening period the insurer that is first notified of the claim has to accept and deal with the claim, with the cost of settlement being shared equally between the two companies.

What is covered by buildings insurance
Most buildings insurance policies cover the main building, including fixtures and fittings (such as fixed bathroom furniture),

garages, domestic outbuildings, fences, paths, drives and patios. Underground pipes for which the policyholder is responsible will also be covered. Certain policies also include ornamental gardens, including plants, hedges and trees; with others, cover for these items is optional or may be offered as part of a contents insurance contract. It is normal for paths, drives, patios and fences to be excluded from the policy as far as subsidence is concerned unless the main property is damaged as well.

Anyone with a greenhouse or swimming pool or other expensive constructions and equipment should check with their broker or insurer to discover the extent of cover. If a property is extended in any way, with a conservatory or additional bedroom, for example, it will obviously be necessary to inform the insurance company and adapt the policy accordingly.

Liability cover
Buildings insurance also covers the policyholder's liabilities as a property owner. This means the insurer will pay any claims made against the policyholder in respect of death, injury or damage to property caused by accidents occurring on or about the property. The maximum pay-out will normally be £1m, although some policies go as high as £5m. The policyholder's legal fees will also be met by the policy. This cover does not extend to members of the policyholder's family or other people living permanently in the house, or to employees of the policyholder.

Other protection
If the building is damaged as a result of an insured peril, it is highly likely that some sort of cleaning-up operation will be necessary. Repairs and rebuilding work may well be complicated and time-consuming. Buildings policies will pay for demolition and for the removal of debris and for any necessary reports by surveyors, engineers and architects. However, if you do arrange for such work to be carried out, it is vital to ensure that recognized professionals are used and that their charges are in line with the

guidelines laid down by (and freely available from) their professional associations. If bills are excessive, the insurer may refuse to pay.

The policy should also pay for the cost of alternative accommodation if the insured property is uninhabitable following the incident. Landlords should also be able to claim for any rent lost because tenants have to move out. However, the insurance company will impose a limit – usually a percentage (such as 10% or 20%) of the sum insured – on the amount it will pay towards these costs.

Non-standard buildings risks
In insurance jargon, 'non-standard' describes properties that are in some way unusual. Some companies prefer normal (or 'standard') business and will not quote for unusual risks, while others specialize in the non-standard sector. If you have a non-standard property, you may have to shop around to find the cover you need. And, as you might expect, you should be prepared to pay a higher rate.

High-value properties may present a problem to some insurers simply because they do not have the resources to cover the risk. In other words, they will not provide cover because a claim would make too big a dent in their kitty. Similarly, non-standard construction puts off a lot of insurers, especially if the materials used in the construction increase the risk of fire or storm damage. Thatched properties and those with a large proportion of timber used in the construction will therefore be considered non-standard by most firms.

Listed properties may also be a problem because any rebuilding work will probably have to be done in the exact style of the original, which inevitably makes a significant difference to the cost. Owners of Grade 1 listed buildings have been required to find identical materials – even down to the types of nails used – when rebuilding the property.

Most of the companies that sell direct prefer standard risks, so if property is at all unusual you will probably be better off going to a broker, who will be able to put you in touch with one of the specialist insurers.

Contents Insurance

If buildings insurance covers the fabric of a property, contents insurance covers what is within. This includes household goods, personal effects and cash belonging to the policyholder and his or her family.

As with buildings insurance, you need to choose a sum insured, which is the maximum amount the policy will pay out in the event of a claim. It is a good idea to make a comprehensive list of all your belongings, giving your best estimate of what they would cost to replace. Many people are shocked when they discover how much their contents are worth; they choose a low sum insured, and are then disappointed when they make a claim.

Some insurers offer 'bedroom-rated' contents policies, which means that houses with a certain number of rooms are automatically insured for a certain amount (the company will have worked out what it thinks is the appropriate figure in each case). This type of policy offers a straightforward method of calculating the sum insured, and also helps to avoid under-insurance because the insurance company sets minimum levels for the sum insured. There will also be a maximum sum insured of somewhere between £30,000 and £50,000, so if you cram a lot of expensive gear into a house with only a modest number of bedrooms, it could well be worth getting a traditional sort of policy.

All policies, bedroom-rated or otherwise, will have a minimum sum insured. They usually start at £7,500 or £10,000. Those with few possessions, such as students, are often put off buying insurance because they do not have goods to this value. While students can probably find the required cover through a specialist company such as Endsleigh, others may need an insurance broker to find the right policy.

In addition to the size of the sum insured, various other factors will affect the contents premium.

Location

Contents policies cover a wide range of perils. While many of these, such as fire or water damage, are considered universal threats, the risk of theft varies dramatically according to where the property is located; those living in areas with a high incidence of crime will find themselves paying significantly more than those living where burglary is not as common. In crude terms, properties in inner city areas and town centres will generally attract higher premiums than those in suburban districts, which in turn will be more expensive to insure than properties in rural areas. However, there may be sharp differences within the same city, which again will be related to the level and the type of reported crime.

Insurers actually decide on which premium rate to apply on the basis of the crime figures for particular post-codes, so even relatively close neighbours may notice significant variations in their insurance costs. If a particular post-code area in the heart of a city is relatively free from crime, its premium levels will go down; by the same token, a rural area plagued by crime will be rated accordingly.

Security

With crime playing such an important part in the calculation of contents insurance premiums, the level of security protecting the house is an important consideration. If certain crime-prevention steps are taken, although an insurance company will still apply the same premium rate to the risk as with any other property in the area, it would provide discounts. Measures might include the installation of a burglar alarm and/or security lighting, the fitting of door and window locks as specified by your insurance company, and membership of a neighbourhood watch scheme. You may even be able to secure a better quote if you have a dog.

Some insurers will also look more favourably on a risk if the house is normally occupied during the day. They have identified certain groups, such as old people and those who have retired, as suitable for special deals. However, those who routinely leave their house unoccupied for lengthy periods or are known to be away from the house at certain times will tend to pay more.

If the sum insured is particularly high, the insurance company may insist on undertaking a security survey and may subsequently insist that certain measures are taken before it will agree to cover the property. You may find that you have to fit an alarm, locks, security lights or join your local neighbourhood watch in order to get cover with some companies. If you already have such items installed, you may earn a discount of, perhaps, 5% for each one.

Excesses

Policyholders can reduce their premiums by opting to pay an excess, which represents the first part of any claim. For example, if a policy carries a £100 excess and a claim is made for £750, the insurer will only pay out £650. The higher the excess, the greater the reduction in premium, although there will be an upper limit on the size of the excess that can be selected. Some policies include a compulsory excess of, say, £50.

Type of cover

There are two types of cover, one significantly more expensive than the other. The costlier version is variously called 'new-for-old', 'reinstatement' or 'replacement-as-new' cover. As these names suggest, this cover provides for insured items to be replaced with new ones or reinstated to the standard of new ones. Some insurers exclude certain items, such as clothing, from this level of cover. If you make a claim under this type of cover, you may find that the insurance company is keen to have items repaired rather than replaced with new ones. This is one of the ways in which they are trying to save money.

The effects of inflation mean that your sum insured might gradually lag behind actual prices and therefore become insufficient to fund the replacement of items on a new-for-old basis. Where this is the case, the insurer may make deductions in what it is prepared to pay out for wear and tear that has occurred. In a bid to help sums insured keep pace with inflation, insurers allow the policy to be linked to the Retail Prices Index.

The second type of cover, which is no longer widely available, is known as 'indemnity terms' or simply 'replacement' cover. This is where the policy is designed to restore the policyholder to the same situation as before the loss occurred; deductions are therefore made for wear and tear on each item before the claim is settled. This option is the cheaper of the two.

However, new-for-old cover is the most popular and should be bought if at all possible. The larger sums paid out on the new-for-old basis mean that it will be much easier to find items you are happy with and to get things back to normal.

Whichever type of cover is taken, it is sensible to keep receipts of purchase for any items of particular value. These can speed up the claims process by confirming which goods have been lost and their exact value.

Your policy should protect you against accidental damage to your possessions – if you spill paint on the carpet or drop a vase, for example. However, the excesses levied on policies are intended to deter you from making a claim every time you drop a wine glass or a piece of crockery. If a video recorder is damaged because a toddler fed banana skins where the tapes should go, you will be insured, but you would not receive a pay-out if you put your foot through the television screen simply because you didn't like the programme.

Valuable items

Most contents policies require valuable items to be listed separately. Some insurers specify a certain cash value – such as £1,500 or £2,000 – above which an item will be defined as 'valuable';

others specify a maximum percentage of the sum insured – usually 5% – that can apply to any single item. Additionally, the insurer may state that no more than, say, 25% of the sum insured will apply to valuables. Valuables include top-of-the-range home entertainment systems, cameras, computers, musical instruments, jewellery and precious metals, furs, antiques, works of art and collections. It is essential that regular, independent valuations are carried out where there is any possibility of dispute over how much an item or collection is worth. Additional premiums may be levied and certain security measures required if valuables are to be included within the contents policy. Particularly valuable items may require separate cover.

Antiques, works of art and collections of very high value may have to be insured with a specialist company through a broker. However, the principal contents insurer should be made aware of their existence, even if they are not included within the contents policy, because your property may be viewed as more attractive to burglars. Some policyholders have submitted claims on their contents policy only to have them rejected on the basis that they had not supplied all the relevant information.

The simple rule is, if in doubt, either ask the broker or the insurer, or make a note on your proposal form. Then, if there is a dispute at a later stage, you can at least say that you never tried to hide anything.

Policy extensions
While contents policies cover most things, there are certain risks that require additional premiums. In other words, you pay a bit more to extend the scope of the policy. If you have a top-of-the-range contract, more cover will be offered as standard. Extensions include:

● **Pedal cycles.** You will be expected to choose an insured value for your cycles and supply frame numbers. An excess may be payable for each bike and cover may only be provided on the basis that you keep the cycles themselves locked or kept in a locked building. Bikes will not normally be covered while in use away from the property. While most policies offer cover for cycles, a cash limit is often imposed – typically £250 – so those with more expensive machines might be better off buying a separate cycle insurance policy.

- **Caravans and their contents.** The insurer may only extend cover to the caravan while it is parked at the insured property or on an approved caravan or camping site (cover while it is being towed will normally be provided by a normal car motor insurance policy). There may also be restrictions on the value of the caravan and its contents and an excess may be required, along with the implementation of certain security measures. Separate caravan policies are available if the house contents policy proves too restrictive. Such a contract would be necessary if the caravan were ever let out to other people, which invalidates the cover provided by the contents policy.

- **Marine craft.** Again, the contents insurer may only be willing to insure craft up to a certain size and in certain locations and may impost an excess and security requirements. Expensive navigational equipment on the boat may be excluded, which might make a specific marine policy more appropriate.

- **Contents of freezers.** This is cover against the possibility that food might deteriorate following the accidental breakdown of the freezer unit or a power cut.

- **Replacement locks if keys are lost or stolen.**

- **Credit cards and cash.** There will normally be a limit of £500 on such losses and an excess of £25 or £50 will probably be payable.

- **Personal accident cover.** This provides for the payment of a lump sum or regular benefit if the policyholder (or others named under the policy) is killed or injured in an accident. The size of the benefit will determine the size of the premium.

- **Legal expenses insurance.** This pays the policyholder's costs (or those of his or her family) in criminal or civil actions; if the action is unsuccessful and costs are awarded to the opposing party, the insurance will also cover this. It will not, however, pay any fines imposed on the policyholder. Cover will not normally be provided for cases of which the policyholder was aware at the time the insurance was taken out.
- **'All risks' insurance.** This is designed to plug the gaps created by exclusions within the main policy. The main benefit is that portable items can be covered while they are outside the property; thus items like cameras and personal steroes can be covered, even when they are taken on holiday. However, there may be a restriction on the length of time that items will be covered while they are outside the UK; this may be 30, 60 or 90 days, depending on the policy.

Pets: It is not normally possible to insure pets under a household contents policy, although some contracts will cover damage caused to contents by pets. Separate pet insurance is available which will reimburse owners for the costs of veterinary treatment and also cover the owner's liabilities in connection with the animal (see Chapter 9, page 108).

Liability

While buildings insurance covers the policyholder's liabilities as owner of the property, contents insurance takes care of liabilities as occupier. This means the policy will pay legal costs and damages resulting from claims made against the policyholder following accidents within or around the house, up to a limit of £1m or £5m, depending on the policy.

Most contents policy liability sections will cover the policyholder for legal liabilities incurred anywhere in the world, although certain exclusions will apply – for instance, accidents arising out of the business or profession of the insured or as the result of the insured being in control of a vehicle.

Non-standard risks

As with buildings insurance, some policies are targeted at 'standard' risks while others are tailored for the 'non-standard' market. Again, non-standard policyholders may find themselves searching harder and paying more for their cover.

Business use

Many insurers remain wary of householders who run their business from home, although attitudes are gradually changing as the number of home-workers grows. Some companies are happy to insure 'white collar' businesses that do not involve machinery or the storage of stock, while others will offer comprehensive cover to virtually any business.

Those working from home have in some cases experienced difficulties in obtaining cover because computers and equipment may be too valuable for a standard contents policy. What is more, insurance companies suggest such items are likely to attract thieves, thus increasing the risk profile of the property as a whole.

As with works of art and valuable collections, it is important for the policyholder to inform the contents insurer of the existence and nature of any business conducted on the premises. Some home-workers have simply not insured their work-related equipment, assuming that their contents policy would replace normal domestic items if they were stolen or damaged; but in many cases the insurance company has turned down the whole claim because the policyholder did not disclose all the relevant information.

Those who, as part of their employment, occasionally work from home should be able to insure computers or other equipment (used partly but not exclusively for the purpose) under a traditional policy, although they may need to be listed as valuables. If the equipment is supplied by the employer, its commercial insurance should cover the items, but it is always a good idea to tell the private contents insurer about any items kept on the premises.

Those running their own businesses may choose to buy a policy that provides cover for loss of profits following a claim, employer's liability cover and protection for equipment when it is away from the property. These are often beyond the scope of traditional contents contracts and need a dedicated policy. It is likely that any unusual risk of this nature will require the services of an independent adviser; most of the companies that sell direct prefer standard business because applications can be easily processed. However, the large number of companies operating in the house contents insurance arena means that more companies will begin to compete for different types of risk, which should have a beneficial impact on insurance premiums.

Making a claim

Insurers complain that a significant number of claims on house contents policies are fraudulent. They suggest that people who, in the normal course of events, are perfectly law-abiding and decent citizens, often exaggerate or fabricate a claim because they think of the insurance company as fair game. There is probably some truth in this; after all, how many times have we heard someone say: 'Well, I've been paying premiums all these years and never had anything out of them, so this is just setting things to rights.'

Actually, it isn't setting things to rights at all. When you pay your premium for a year's cover, you simply buy cover for that year. If you do not make a claim, you have still enjoyed the benefit of the cover. You have not lodged a deposit with the insurance company that you should try to recoup at some later stage when you get the chance. So when you make a claim, be honest, if only because there is an increasing risk of your being caught. The insurance community has set up the Claims Underwriting Exchange, which allows information on policyholders and their claims records to be pooled and suspicious claims to be investigated. If you get caught making a fraudulent claim, the insurance company is likely to take you to court to persuade you that you are guilty of criminal behaviour.

When you claim, you may also receive a visit from a loss adjuster, appointed by the insurance company to check whether a claim is justified and accurate. Adjusters are impartial, and are obliged by their professional code to concentrate on finding the right figure, rather than simply knocking down your estimate. This means the adjuster might even advise you to increase your claim.

If you feel it necessary, you can appoint a loss assessor to represent you in your dealings with the adjuster and the insurance company. Remember also that your broker, if you have one, should work on your behalf to smooth the claims process.

3 ‖ *Motor Insurance*

No matter how much sense it makes to have life insurance, no one can force you to take out a policy. And if you want to risk having no insurance on your house and possessions, that is up to you. But if you take a motor vehicle on the road, you have no choice: by law – the Road Traffic Act, to be precise – you must insure yourself against the possibility that you might be involved in an accident with someone else.

Insurers call that 'someone else' the 'third party', a phrase you will come across in most motor insurance policies. In addition to this basic form of protection, it is also possible to insure yourself and your own vehicle by choosing a policy that is more comprehensive in scope. Obviously, the more cover offered by the policy, the more expensive it will be.

As with other forms of insurance, a battle has broken out in the motor market between traditional brokers and companies that sell direct over the telephone. For many people, this is helping to drive down the cost of motor insurance. But to be sure you are getting the best deal you have to know what sort of policies are on offer: be prepared to shop around, contacting both brokers and direct insurers to find the best price and the best level of service.

The main options open to drivers are:

- **Third party only cover.** This covers you if you cause an accident that results in injury to a third party or damage to a third party's property. This is the cheapest type of cover but it is not widely sold because it offers no protection to you as the driver or against damage or theft of your car.

- **Third party, fire and theft.** This type of policy takes care of the legal obligations you owe to third parties and also, as its name suggests, provides for your vehicle to be repaired or replaced if it catches fire or is stolen. This is a low-cost policy, popular with those who do not want to pay the higher premiums necessary for fully comprehensive cover.
- **Comprehensive.** This policy includes the required cover for third party risks and also insures the driver's vehicle against fire, theft and any other accidental loss or damage. This means that if you cause an accident, the policy will pay for the repair or replacement of your vehicle as well as that of the other person.

Cost Factors

The price you pay for motor insurance is determined by a host of things, some of which are in your control, some which are not. Whether you buy from a broker or direct from an insurance company, you will be asked certain questions about yourself and your car. When you ask for a quote, your details are fed into a computer. This is programmed by the insurance company according to its own judgement. If it thinks you represent a good risk, it will deliver a low price. If, on the other hand, it has suffered a lot of claims from people like you, it will quote a higher premium.

It is important to be as accurate as possible when providing information for a quotation. If you deliberately answer questions incorrectly or fail to disclose information when requested, you may invalidate your cover completely: if you were to be involved in an accident, you would have to bear all the costs yourself.

The age and experience of the driver

Insurance companies tend to reward experienced drivers with lower premiums, especially if their driving history is free from accidents and convictions for motoring offences. People under a certain age – normally 25 – are classified as 'young drivers' and deemed to present a greater risk. They will therefore be required to pay higher premiums or, in extreme cases, refused cover altogether.

Older drivers can experience similar difficulties. Once drivers reach a certain age – the figure varies from insurer to insurer but might be as low as 55 – premiums start to increase again. This is because older people generally have slower reactions and are therefore considered to be more at risk than younger drivers.

As an individual, you might fizz with resentment because you feel confident that you drive better than others in your age group. But the insurers rely on Government statistics on the proportion of people from different groups that are involved in accidents. Once you fall into a certain category, there is little you can do except shop around for a company willing to adopt a more sympathetic approach.

Sex

Your sex can also influence the size of your premium. An increasing number of companies are offering cheaper cover to women because, according to the official statistics, they are a better insurance risk. The debate whether men or women are the better drivers will probably never be resolved, but the figures suggest that the overwhelming majority of accidents are caused by men. In 1993 204,000 male drivers were involved in such accidents while the figure for women was 95,000. Only a third of road injury accidents in 1994 involved women.

Home Office figures reiterate the pro-women arguments: men are 13 times more likely to commit a motoring offence, so of every 100 people convicted, only seven will be women. And it seems that, the more serious the offence, the more likely the presence of testosterone as a determining factor: 98% of deaths from dangerous driving, 95% of reckless driving cases and 95% of drunk driving incidents involve men. According to the RAC, women are half as likely as men to jump a red light and only 1% of women find speed exciting, compared with 40% of 'boy racers' (93% of speeding cases involve men).

Of course, a lot of the driving done by women is during the day, between the dangerous rush hours, rather than in them. They tend to drive fewer miles and have accidents at slower speeds and anyway drive smaller cars, all of which improves their insurance profile.

The type of vehicle and its age

As you might expect, it costs more to insure a fast, expensive car than a relatively inexpensive, sedate saloon. In assessing the risk of particular vehicles, insurers have come up with 20 vehicle groupings to cover every mass-produced car built since 1960. When deciding which car should go into which category, they take into account price, age, maximum speed, rate of acceleration, the availability of spares and the number and distribution of authorized repair facilities. Saloons of modest value and similar vehicles would go into one of the lower groups; pricey high-performance cars would go into a higher group.

Unusual cars and rare, vintage vehicles will often not be allocated to a particular group. If this is the case, the insurer may not be able to provide a quote. However, some firms specialize in insuring this type of vehicle and will use their own figures to calculate the appropriate premium.

Where the driver lives

Another rule of thumb for motor insurance is that, the more densely populated the area where the motorist lives, the higher the premium will be. There are two reasons for this: if there are more people in an area, there will be more cars on the road and a greater likelihood of road accidents, and the risk of the vehicle being stolen is greater. So drivers in cities tend to pay more than those in rural areas. The statistics used by insurers are very precise, however, so two areas in the same city may see wide variations in premium levels because of the difference in car crime. In the worst areas insurers may even decline to offer a quotation unless certain security measures, such as keeping the car in a garage overnight or fitting an alarm or immobilizer, are implemented.

The driver's occupation
The driver's occupation can influence the premium even when the car is not used for work or business purposes. Among those who might find their premiums increased (or 'loaded', as insurers call it) because of their jobs are publicans, journalists, entertainers and sportsmen, who are considered more of a risk because they tend to drink more than people in other professions and their cars are likely to be left unattended for lengthy periods, often at night.

How the vehicle will be used
Insurers have two main classes of use for private cars and charge different prices according to which category is applicable:

- **Social, domestic and pleasure (SD&P).** This is the cheapest and most common option. If you have this type of cover, you cannot hire your car out to someone else or use it for commercial travelling; nor can you use it for racing or other competitions. However, it can be used in connection with your business and that of your employer, and it can be used for travelling to and from work. Some companies offer an even cheaper version of SD&P that excludes all business use except commuting.
- **Social, domestic and pleasure and use for the business of the insured and his or her employer or partner.** The difference between this class and straightforward SD&P is that the use of the vehicle by other people is not restricted, which means an employee can use the car in connection with the business. Some policies will allow commercial travelling.

The type of cover
As mentioned earlier, third party only cover is cheaper than third party, fire and theft, which is in turn cheaper than comprehensive cover.

No claims discounts (or NCD)

If you do not claim on your policy, your insurer will reward you with a discount off your premium. The longer you go without making a claim, the greater the discount will be until it reaches the maximum amount. These no claims discounts (or no claims bonuses, as they are sometimes known) take the form of a percentage reduction in the premium, as shown in Table 5.

Table 5: Typical no claims discount

Years without claim	Discount off gross premium
1	20%
2	30%
3	40%
4	50%
5	60%

Some insurers offer a one-year discount of 25%, stepping up to a maximum of 65%.

Clearly, three or four years' NCD can make a significant difference to the size of a premium. Many drivers with comprehensive cover prefer to pay for minor repairs out of their own pocket in order not to jeopardize their entitlement to a discount. Many insurance companies acknowledge this by offering 'protected' NCDs. This is where, for an extra premium, you can insure your discount against a set number of claims occurring within a certain period. Typically, the insurer will allow two claims within a three-year period without harming your entitlement to a no claims discount.

Depending on the insurance company, a claim might send you back to zero discount or it might just knock you two or three steps down the discount ladder. Drivers who are particularly accident-prone, however, can expect to see their entitlement to a discount disappear completely. Those with particularly poor driving records may even see their premium being 'loaded' as a result, like an NCD in reverse.

The fact that you have built up an NCD with one company should not discourage you from shopping around for a better deal when it is time to renew. Insurers will recognize any NCD entitlement from a rival company but it will insist on proof. This will normally be supplied by the old company but it may take time to come through, so it is always a good idea not to leave it to the last minute.

Excesses (or deductibles)

The 'policy excess' included in many motor insurance contracts – sometimes referred to as a 'deductible' – is the contribution made by the policyholder towards the cost of a claim. The excess comes in two forms: mandatory and voluntary. If your policy includes a mandatory excess, you have to pay it, so it is worth checking when you arrange your cover so that you don't get a nasty surprise when you make a claim. By choosing to pay a voluntary excess, you obtain a reduction in the premium: the larger the excess, the lower the premium. Drivers with poor driving records or with costly or high-performance cars will often be faced with a compulsory excess.

Excesses normally start at £50 or £100 but may rise to £500 or even higher when particularly expensive vehicles are involved.

Security factors

Insurers have become increasingly concerned about the amount of money they are having to pay out because of auto-crime. Drivers have also grown weary of seeing their vehicles and their possessions stolen. This has prompted a general increase in interest in vehicle security: drivers who take extra care of their vehicles can now secure reductions in their motor insurance premiums. You could conclude, on the other hand, that those who are lax about security are being penalized with higher premiums.

Insurers will quote lower rates if a vehicle is fitted with an alarm and/or an immobilizing device or if it is kept in a garage overnight rather than left on the street. Discounts may also be available if the policyholder completes a specified advanced driver training course sometimes known as a 'defensive' driver training course. This takes two or three hours to complete and there is usually no 'pass' or 'fail' – simply completing the course is enough to earn the discount. If your insurance company is willing to offer a discount to those who take such a course, it may well be able to put you in touch with organizations that run them. A decent motor broker will also have details of how to proceed.

Other drivers

When obtaining a quotation, you will be asked who else will be driving the car. If use is restricted to you or you plus spouse (or partner), the premium will not be unduly affected, but if others, particularly children, are included, the premiums may be increased to reflect the greater risks.

Illness

Some insurers charge more if policyholders suffer from conditions such as diabetes or epilepsy. Again, some companies specialize in providing cover in such cases, but some simply refuse to offer cover to people with these ailments. By and large, it is best to go to a broker if you suffer from either of these conditions since most of the companies that sell direct prefer 'standard' risks. However, direct insurers are expanding their fields of interest all the time, so 'non-standard' risks should soon have a good selection of direct insurers keen to offer them protection.

Standard and non-standard risks

Insurance companies often refer to the 'standard' and 'non-standard' motor markets. The standard market covers roughly three-quarters of all drivers, while the non-standard market is made up of the six million others who are considered to be in a higher risk category by virtue of their age, their car, their occupation, their health or their driving record (including convictions).

Non-standard motorists have always faced higher premiums and struggled in some instances to find cover at any price. Recently, however, a number of companies have targeted the non-standard sector, a move which is leading to more competitive premiums and greater availability of cover. As mentioned above, several direct insurance companies are now challenging the dominance of brokers in the non-standard sector of the market.

Instalments

Motor insurance premiums, especially for comprehensive policies, are often so large that it may be difficult to pay them in one go. Most insurers have therefore introduced instalment schemes, whereby payment is made each month, usually by standing order. When arranging to pay by instalment, it is important to check the details. Some companies levy an additional charge, typically 5% or 6%, in return for the credit facility; others impose no charge.

While most motor policies last for 12 months, it is also possible to arrange six- and even three-month periods of cover. This can be a useful way to reduce the size of the initial premium, but you may find that four quarterly policies ultimately work out more expensive than one annual one.

Motorcycle Insurance

Many of the factors determining the price of motor insurance also apply to motor cycle insurance. Insurers are particularly wary of younger, male drivers of bigger bikes and will 'load' such risks heavily, so many people have to settle for third party or third party, fire and theft cover rather than the superior comprehensive option.

As with cars, premiums will also be affected by claims history, place of residence, convictions, excesses and security measures. Until recently, NCD entitlements were a rarity in the motorcycle insurance market, but a number of insurers have started to introduce them as a way of rewarding conscientious policyholders.

While motor insurance is now often sold direct by insurance companies, motorcycle insurance is still sold predominantly by brokers.

Making a Claim

If you are involved in an accident and think it likely that you will make a claim or a claim will be made against you, you should tell the insurance company straight away. Not only does prompt action get the insurance wheels in motion; it may mean you can take advantage of the emergency assistance offered by many policies – maybe a mechanic or even a replacement vehicle. Similarly, if any police or legal proceedings are pending, you should notify your insurer without delay.

If you are involved in an accident that you think will result in a claim, remember the following rules:

- Get the name and address of the other person or people involved, making a note of the registration number and the make of their car(s).
- Get the name of their insurance company. If they have their policy with them, take down the policy number.
- Do not discuss whose fault the accident was: it could cause problems at a later stage.
- Get the name and address of any independent witnesses.
- If in doubt, call the police.
- If you have a camera or video recorder in the car, get pictures before the vehicles are moved. At the very least, make a sketch while the details are fresh in your mind.
- Above all, remain calm: no amount of ranting, raving or bemoaning your bad luck will turn the clock back to before the accident happened.

If you bought your cover through a broker, you should let the broker handle the communications with the insurance company – that is why you are paying a commission. If there has been an accident, you will be required to complete a claims form giving details of the incident. This will help your insurance company and the insurance company of the other person to decide who, if anyone, was at fault and how the claim should be settled. Again, supplying false information is likely to invalidate cover and may lead to criminal proceedings.

If your car needs repairs, ask your insurance company for advice. It may have a network of recommended repairers and you should take your car to one of these if at all possible as it will probably be cheaper and quicker. If the insurer has no special arrangements, go to two or three competent garages and ask for estimates. Send this to your insurer – do not simply tell the garage to get on with it; the repairs must be authorized by the insurer first.

Travelling Abroad

The opening of the Channel Tunnel is expected to increase the number of UK drivers taking their cars to Europe. If you decide to venture abroad, it is essential that you have adequate insurance cover.

Within most of Europe and certain parts of North Africa, it is possible for UK policyholders to extend their insurance to all other countries in this region through the Green Card system. This guarantees that cover meets the minimum requirements of the country being visited. Some insurers provide a Green Card with every policy they sell, while others will supply one on request. Some will charge an additional fee (usually £15) when doing so. It can take some time for the Green Card to come through, so if you are planning a trip abroad, you should leave plenty of time to make the necessary arrangements. If you go abroad frequently, you should consider your Green Card arrangements when you take out cover or renew your policy.

Those driving their own vehicles outside Europe should check their insurance obligations before leaving the UK. It is not un-known for travellers to be turned back by border guards if they do not have the necessary documentation or to be charged high levies by officials who take the opportunity to 'arrange' cover for them.

If you are driving a hire car, the hire company should ensure that adequate cover is in place.

Different countries (and, within some countries, different states or regions) have different expectations of road-users. Some, like the UK, tolerate a certain level of alcohol consumption; others will penalize a driver who has consumed any alcohol at all. In some countries you may turn right through a red light when road conditions allow. Unenlightened drivers from the UK may sit in some confusion wondering what they have done to merit such horn-blowing and fist-waving. So it is a good idea to acquaint yourself with the driving laws of any country you visit. If your travel agent is unable to help, the relevant embassy should give you the necessary information.

Caravans

If you tow a caravan or a trailer with your car, you will normally be covered automatically for any liabilities you may incur if you cause an accident. However, if you want to protect yourself against damage to the vehicle you are towing, or if you want separate protection for the vehicle while it is not being towed, you will need a separate policy.

The minimum requirement of a caravan policy is protection against accidental damage, fire, theft, storm, flood and vandalism. More expensive policies might also offer cover for trips abroad and provide a cash sum to pay for alternative accommodation if the vehicle is uninhabitable while you are on holiday. You should also check what happens if your caravan is damaged away from its normal base: does the policy pay for the cost of transportation, repair and storage?

Bear in mind that any belongings you take with you in the caravan from your normal residence may be covered under the all-risks section of your house contents policy. Check this contract

Table 6: Caravan insurance: sample costs for 'new for old' cover on vehicles up to 5 years old

Model	Cost of structure	Contents	Premium
Elldis Storm 1994	£14,000	£1,000	£353,63
Swift Corniche 1991	£7,500	£1,000	£203,72
Lunar Clubman 1988	£5,000	£1,000	£146.06

Source: Independent Insurance

and any caravan insurance you might have to see whether there is an overlap. Any items that are kept permanently in the caravan will need to be covered by the caravan policy's contents section.

You can buy caravan insurance through insurance brokers or through organizations such as the Caravan Club and the Caravan & Camping Club.

Getting the Best Deal

With well over 20 million cars and motorcycles on the road in the UK, motor insurance is big business and many insurance companies and intermediaries are competing for a slice of the annual £7 billion premium cake. This is good news for the consumer as it helps to keep premiums down, but it is still important to shop around to get the best deal.

The bulk of motor insurance is sold by consultants and brokers, but insurance companies which sell direct to the public are winning an increasing share of the market. Shopping around among both types of supplier is a good idea because, while most brokers can obtain quotations from a wide range of companies, they will not give you details of policies sold by the direct insurers; and a company selling direct will only provide information on its own contracts. Try to obtain quotes from a broker and two or three direct insurers in order to make sure that you have 'covered the market'. The difference in premiums can stretch into hundreds of pounds, so this will be time well invested.

4 ‖ *Medical Insurance*

Since 1948 the UK has been blessed with a National Health Service that is designed to provide free medical treatment on demand to anyone who requires it. It has always been possible, however, to 'go private' and pay for treatment. And, as the NHS has come under increasing pressure because of high demand and low resources, the private option has become more popular.

Many people prefer private treatment because it allows them to by-pass waiting lists and to have their treatment when it suits them. Appointments can be arranged around work and family commitments instead of being fitted into the rigid timetable enforced by the NHS hospital and doctors. Indeed, paying for your care allows you to choose where and by whom you will be looked after. The current NHS policy of developing centres of excellence in certain hospitals mean that many people are having to travel further for treatment. If you can afford to pay, however, you increase your choice of location. Moreover, you will receive a greater degree of privacy and comfort than is afforded to NHS patients. Creature comforts like your own television and radio and being able to have visitors at any time can make a big difference.

The problem with paying for your medical treatment, of course, is that it can be extremely expensive. Everything associated with private medicine costs a lot of money, from the drugs and equipment to the highly skilled and experienced staff. And prices are rising: inflation in medical costs is rising at over 12% compared to 3% elsewhere in the economy. This is why very few of us are able to pay for our private medical care out of ready cash. Unusually we can only afford to go private if we have taken out private medical insurance (PMI) to cover the costs. But under the PMI banner there are a range of policies to suit different needs and different pockets. It is therefore worth assessing what is on offer and matching it to your particular circumstances.

Cover through work
The first question to ask is whether you receive medical insurance as a benefit of your job. Some employers provide free cover to staff and their families: if employees are off sick, it is in the best interests of the company that they are well looked after and back at work as soon as possible. The flexibility offered by the private sector is seen as the best way of ensuring this.

It should be noted that medical insurance is a taxable benefit. In other words, if your employer provides you with medical insurance, you will pay income tax on the value of the premiums paid by the company on your behalf. Tax nothwithstanding, medical cover is generally reckoned to be one of the most valuable perks there is. Not everyone, though, is lucky enough to have it. Those who have to buy insurance out of their own pocket have a range of organizations from which to choose, so – as ever with insurance – it is best to shop around.

The PMI Providers

The big name in the PMI market has for years been the British United Provident Association, better known as BUPA. This huge organization runs hospitals and provides insurance to companies and individuals. At the height of its popularity, it insured nearly 8 out of every 10 people who had medical cover. As a company limited by guarantee whose primary purpose is the administration of a provident fund BUPA does not have shareholders. This means that any profits made by the organization are ploughed back into the business for the health care needs of its members rather than distributed as dividends.

Two other provident associations, Private Patients Plan (PPP) and Western Provident Association (WPA), have gradually increased their share of the market. BUPA has also faced competition from traditional insurance companies such as Norwich Union and Cornhill. All this activity has served to broaden the selection of policies on offer.

Medical insurers sell direct to the public and through insurance brokers and other consultants. Just as with other forms of insurance, it is the job of the broker to shop around on your behalf to find the most suitable policy at the best price. And if you have to make a claim, the broker should deal with the insurance company to ensure that things go smoothly. Some brokers specialize in medical insurance; others offer medical insurance alongside motor, household and other types of protection. There is nothing wrong with going to an all-rounder like this so long as you are satisfied that you are getting expert advice. If you get the impression that your broker simply funnels all medical insurance enquiries to one particular company without scouring the market, you should seriously consider looking elsewhere.

Some organizations have negotiated special arrangements with particular medical insurance companies and pass on preferential rates to their members and customers. You might therefore be able to secure a good deal through your trade union, professional association or building society. Do not buy blind, however: check what else is available from the leading players to make sure you are getting a good deal. It is important to remember that, when you buy through a middleman, commission will be added to your premiums. Make sure that you are getting value for this money – do not be afraid to ask the broker to justify that commission.

Buying direct

The story of how medical insurance is sold was given a further twist in 1995 when Guardian Direct started selling PMI over the telephone. Previously, anyone wanting cover had to go through a lengthy question and answer process that involved filling in forms and obtaining medical evidence from doctors. In some instances a medical examination would also be required. Guardian has simplified the process so that it is possible to buy cover in the course of one conversation, having answered five simple questions:

- Name and address
- Date of birth
- Occupation
- Smoker/non-smoker
- Details of any existing serious or terminal medical conditions.

The premium is paid for with a credit card during the course of the call and cover commences immediately, either for the individual alone or with the other members of the family. It remains to be seen how successful this venture will be, but if it attracts a lot of customers, it is also likely to spawn a number of imitators. Guardian obviously hopes that cost-savings will help it to offer competitive premiums which will give it an edge over its more traditional rivals.

What is covered

The basic aim of PMI is to cover the cost of treatment for unforeseen illness and injury. But while some comprehensive policies cover virtually every possible cost that might be incurred, other 'budget' schemes only provide for certain charges. Obviously, the more extensive the cover, the bigger the premium.

The main areas of cover are:

- **Professional fees** to pay for consultants, specialist physicians, anaesthetists and surgeons
- **Hospital charges**: the cost of accommodation and nursing, either in a private hospital or in a private bed within an NHS hospital
- **Specialist treatments**, including physiotherapy, chemotherapy, radiology, which may be taken as an in- or outpatient

- **Drugs, tests, X-rays, dressings and treatments**
- **Out-patient treatments**
- **Home nursing**
- **Cash benefit**: a sum (typically £50) which is paid for every night the policyholder receives treatment from the NHS.

Deluxe policies will also pay for the cost of medical treatment undertaken while abroad. This can be worthwhile for frequent travellers, but those who only make the occasional trip may find their travel insurance policy provides adequate protection. If the inclusion of international cover pushes up the premium significantly, you should seriously consider whether you really need it.

Main exclusions and exceptions

Even the most comprehensive PMI policy will carry a hefty list of exclusions. These generally prevent you from claiming for treatments for conditions that existed before you took out the cover* and for problems that are in some way your own fault, such as drug dependence, or to which you can be said to have contributed, such as pregnancy. Routine tests and cosmetic treatments will also be excluded.

The most common exclusions include:

- Fees payable to a general practitioner
- Treatments not recommended by a general practitioner
- Dental treatments (except those requiring an operation)
- Cosmetic surgery (except when made necessary by an accident)
- Routine tests and examinations (such as for sight and hearing)
- Vaccinations

---

* Some policies will cover pre-existing conditions once you have been on cover for a certain amount of time. This period is referred to as the 'moratorium'. If you have an existing problem, ask the insurer whether a moratorium is offered with the policy. Never try to hide a condition from which you currently suffer or from which you have suffered in the past. This is called 'non-disclosure' and may result in your entire claim being rejected.

- Pregnancy and childbirth (although complications arising in pregnancy may be covered)
- Termination of pregnancy
- Infertility treatment
- Self-inflicted injuries
- Alcohol and drug dependence
- AIDS
- Injuries sustained in war.

The cost of PMI

As the questions asked over the telephone by Guardian Direct suggest (see page 57), the main factors affecting how much you pay for your PMI are your age, sex, your occupation, whether or not you are a smoker and your general state of health. The amount of detail required about your medical history will vary depending on the insurer; some will ask you to undergo a medical examination before quoting a price. Your occupation will be taken into account because certain jobs carry a greater risk of injury and illness than others: your PMI premiums will be higher because, in theory, you are more likely to suffer from strains and similar problems that cannot be traced to a specific incident. However, if you are injured in the course of your work through no fault of your own, your employer's insurance should cover the cost of your treatment.

The general scope of a medical insurance policy will also determine how much it costs. For example, some impose limits on how much will be paid out in any one year. This will sometimes be expressed as a cash sum and sometimes as a maximum number of days that can be spent in hospital each year. Insurers strive to avoid situations where their policyholders run out of cover halfway through a course of treatment. Ideally, they like to be aware of the situation before the treatment begins so that they can discuss the potential shortfall with the policyholder. In some circumstances it may be necessary to rely on the NHS if the policy looks like being inadequate.

There may also be a limit on the amount that can be spent on each type of treatment. This would mean, for example, that only a specified amount could be spent on home nursing or on out-patient treatment.

Premium levels will also be affected by the type of hospital attended. Private hospitals are similar to hotels in that they offer a wide selection of prices. If you want to stay in the equivalent of the Ritz or the Savoy, you must expect to pay the appropriate price. The luxury of the accommodation and the quality of the peripheral services will be higher; the quality of your medical treatment will not be affected. Hospital prices fall into 'bands' and PMI policies are designed to pay specific band costs, with the premiums reflecting the policyholder's choice.

The most expensive hospitals tend to be in London and other big urban centres. The location of the hospital is important, and you may be prepared to pay a little extra in order to have access to your nearest hospital so that your family can visit you easily. You may even be willing to settle for rather modest accommodation in order to be in the location you desire. Your insurer might quote prices for three bands of hospital and tell you which hospitals in your area fall into which category.

Some policies are designed to mesh with available NHS services. With this sort of insurance, cover might only be provided when the NHS waiting list is, for example, more than six weeks long. Cover might be available for NHS pay beds, but not for fully private hospitals.

As with motor and household insurance, it is possible to reduce the size of the premium by agreeing to pay the first part of any claim – the 'excess'. The larger the contribution you are prepared to make towards the cost of the claim, the lower the premium will be. However, when selecting the excess, be realistic: there is no point in choosing a higher figure in order to secure a lower premium if you cannot afford to pay up when you make the claim.

It is also worth remembering that PMI is an annual contract that has to be renewed each year, so check your renewal documents: insurance companies reserve the right to change the scope of the cover and to increase the premiums and this is the only time they are obliged to tell you.

Most companies automatically levy premium increases as you reach certain ages, so you might see the cost going up when you reach 30, 40, 50 and so on. Because older people are a worse risk from the medical insurer's point of view, the premium increases may be substantial as you get on, but if you have been with the same insurer for a number of years, the rising premiums are still likely to be less steep than the premiums charged by any new insurer you approached.

One medical insurance company, OHRA UK, differs from most of the market in that it only imposes one age-related premium increase. The 'age-breaks' when the premium increase takes place are 30, 40, 50 and 60. Whatever age you are when you join, you only face a single age-related premium increase – when you reach the next age-break. So if you join at 43, your premiums increase at 50 but not at 60 or thereafter. In the meantime, of course, OHRA premiums might increase to reflect rising costs – but this would be the case with whichever company you bought your cover from.

Remember that medical insurance attracts insurance premium tax, which is charged at 2.5% of the premium.

Making a Claim

Obviously, if you have a medical problem of any kind, the first thing to do is to see your general practitioner. Don't rush straight to a private hospital and demand that they take care of you. If you are likely to need to claim on your PMI, your doctor will be able to arrange the private consultation.

It is vital that you contact your insurer at the earliest possible opportunity, preferably over the telephone. Your policy documents should explain the procedure and will probably give you details of a telephone hot-line set up specifically for this purpose.

Table 7: The costs of private medical insurance

Example (a)
The following quotation is for a married couple; the husband is 32 and the wife 23. They have two children aged 4 and 2. The cost is for a band C hospital; they live in North London. Figures are given for different contracts, reflecting different levels of cover, where appropriate.

Company	Contract	Monthly premium
BUPA	Local Care	£54.57
	Local Hospital Care	£36.41
Guardian Direct	Healthcare	£53.88
OHRA UK	Medios Healthcare	£61.47*
PPP	VIP	£108.60
	Budget	£52.20
Sun Alliance	Family Health	£96.95

* *The premium goes down to £38.42 if the policyholder agrees to bear part of the cost of the claim.*

Example (b)
The following quotation is for a single man aged 30 and 40 using hospitals in different bands.

Age of policyholder (male)	Hospital band	Annual premium	Monthly premium
30	A	£557.50	£48.90
30	B	£361.40	£31.70
30	C	£299.80	£26.30
40	A	£606.50	£53.20
40	B	£404.70	£35.50
40	C	£337.40	£29.60

Source: OHRA UK

As mentioned earlier, not every policy covers every contingency, so you must check with the insurance company to confirm that the diagnosis or treatment is actually covered.

If you are referred to a consultant, you may subsequently be committed to hospital for further treatment. Again, it is vital that the insurance company is kept abreast of the situation so that you do not end up in a hospital from a more expensive price band than your policy allows. If you keep the insurance company fully informed, you won't go far wrong. Of course, if you are ill, the last thing you need is an administrative headache, so make sure that members of your family, friends or perhaps colleagues know where your insurance documents are kept so that they can take on this burden for you. Of course, if you bought your cover through a broker, the liaison with the insurance company should largely be taken care of, but it is as well to have someone close to you keeping an eye on things as well.

When you receive private treatment, you will find yourself with plenty of bills to sign. Try to read through them and relate them to the treatment you receive. Take your time and do not be pressured into hurrying – there may well be a substantial amount of money involved, and you can be sure that the insurance company will go through the bills with a fine-tooth comb. If there is any doubt over the cost of treatment, it is best to identify it at an early stage if possible. Again, it is a great help to have a relative, friend or broker you can rely on.

The hospital bills – those relating to the cost of your accommodation – will often be sent direct to the insurance company. Some hospitals may be owned by the same firm that provides your insurance, in which case this part of the process should be relatively painless. Other bills – those relating to the treatment you have received – may be sent to you personally and should be forwarded to the insurance company immediately.

Tax relief

Tax relief is available at the basic rate on some PMI policies. This means you can save 25% on premiums. In order to qualify, however, the policyholder has to be aged 60 or over when the policy is taken out, although the policyholder does not have to be the person who is paying the premiums, which means that children can pay for cover on behalf of their parents and obtain the cost saving.

Tax relief, of course, should be set against the Insurance Premium Tax that has to be paid on many types of insurance premium. This is calculated at 2.5% of the premium.

Dental insurance

Standard medical insurance policies normally exclude dental work (except treatment required following an accident), but it is possible to buy separate protection. This may be a good idea because the cost of treatment can be very high, even if you use the NHS facilities that still exist.

It is estimated that 10,000 of the country's 27,000 dentists have either gone completely private or have stopped accepting new NHS patients. If you find an NHS dentist, you will have to pay 80% of the cost of treatment, up to a maximum of £250. You only get treatment free if you are on social security benefit or are pregnant. Children also receive free care.

Most dental insurance policies are based on 'capitation'. This simply means that, instead of paying a premium and receiving a benefit that pays for the cost of the treatment you receive, you pay a monthly subscription that entitles you to visit your dentist on a regular basis for free check-ups and any other work that is required. The size of the subscription for a capitation scheme tends to range between £5 and £15 per month, depending on the level of cover and the state of your teeth. If you have dental problems, the cost will inevitably be higher, but if you go to the dentist on a regular basis and your teeth improve as a result, your subscription should come down accordingly; if they deteriorate, it will increase.

These schemes are effectively run by dentists rather than insurance companies, and you join through your dentist. If he or she does not offer such an arrangement, one of the insurance companies (the main players are BUPA, WPA, Private Patients Plan and Norwich Union) will be able to point you in the right direction.

Capitation schemes have limitations: you may, for example, have to pay for the materials used in crowns, bridges and dentures; there might also be a bill if your dentist has to subcontract work to a laboratory; and not every policy will pay for emergency or purely cosmetic work.

Complementary Medicine

An increasing number of medical insurance policies are recognizing the rising popularity of complementary and alternative medicine and will pay the costs of treatments such as osteopathy and chiropractice. However, most policies will only pay for treatment that is recommended by your general practitioner, so it is usually necessary to be given the green light before visiting the specialist.

Many branches of alternative medicine are still viewed with suspicion by the mainstream medical community, including insurance companies, so your policy may stipulate that you visit a properly qualified practitioner. As these treatments become more established, insurers should begin to recognize their merit and offer cover accordingly.

Again, it is essential to check with your insurer to find out the precise terms of your contract. If costs for alternative and complementary medicine are covered, they are likely to be subject to the limits that appear in the out-patients section of the policy.

Hospital Cash Plans

This sort of plan may be provided by an employer that does not want (or cannot afford) to fund full-blown PMI for its workforce. Associations and clubs also provide members with this sort of cover, and it is possible to buy it direct from the company or through a broker. Premiums for an individual can be as low as £2 per month.

Hospital cash plans are very straightforward animals: they pay a cash sum, usually £25 or £50, for every night spent in hospital, regardless of whether it is an NHS or private facility. The money can be used for any purpose – travel expenses for visitors, baby-sitters, and even flowers and chocolates.

Accident and Sickness Insurance

While PMI is designed to pay specific costs associated with medical treatment, accident and sickness insurance pays out a certain amount – usually known as the benefit – when a valid claim is made. Claims can be made in the event of:

- Accidental death
- The loss of a limb
- Disablement
- Hospitalization.

The benefit is paid in a number of ways. In the event of death or the loss of a limb (which includes the loss of sight), or if the policyholder is permanently prevented from working because of disablement suffered in an accident, a cash sum will be paid. If the injury prevents the policyholder from working but is not deemed to be permanently disabling, then a weekly cash payment will be made, usually for a period of two years. With some policies a policyholder who is still disabled after the two years are up will receive the lump sum benefit; if at any point during the payment of the weekly benefit the disability is diagnosed as permanent rather than temporary, the lump sum will be paid and the weekly payments will cease. If the disablement has only a limited impact on the policyholder's life, then a reduced payment may be made.

Some policies also include a nightly cash benefit similar to that paid by hospital cash plans (see above).

Exclusions
As you might expect, insurance companies offering this sort of protection are wary of people who have risky jobs or participate in

dangerous sports such as motor racing, parachuting, hang-gliding, bungee-jumping, mountaineering, pot-holing and sub-aqua. Some policies will simply exclude these activities altogether, which means that if you get injured while participating in that sport, your claim will not be paid.

When arranging this sort of cover, you *must* read through the list of exclusions. Proposal forms often ask: 'Do you participate in any of the following activities?' and list sports like those just mentioned. The onus is on the policyholder to provide accurate information upon which the premium calculation will be based. As with all forms of insurance, be as honest as possible when answering questions of this sort.

Payment of an additional premium will often extend the scope of a policy to include dangerous activities, although those with what the insurers would term a 'high risk profile' might find it cheaper to take out a specially designed contract. This will almost certainly be the case if you are able to buy cover through a club, which can negotiate a good deal with the insurance company.

An extension of the accident and sickness insurance is permanent health insurance (PHI) – or income replacement cover, as it is sometimes known. This type of protection will be explained in the next chapter.

5 | *Income Replacement Insurance*

If a regular pay cheque helps you maintain your lifestyle, how would you cope without it? This is the question you should ask yourself when contemplating whether you need an income replacement insurance policy.

If you were to suffer an accident or become seriously ill, life would be bad enough; and how much worse if your affliction or injury prevented you from earning an income. The bills would certainly keep coming in: the mortgage, electricity, gas and water charges would still have to be paid, you would still have to buy essentials like food and clothing, and you would still be liable for council tax. And what about the cost of running the car, or going on holiday? These are just a few of the financial commitments that could turn a bad situation into an unbearable one.

Few of us recognize the threat to our standards of living posed by the inability to earn an income due to illness or accident, but the statistics are alarming: one in five of us will be off work for three months through disability at some point in our career. At any given time, over one million people have been claiming State invalidity support for over a year, and of these, over 600,000 have been sick or disabled for longer than three years. A 40-year-old man is six times more likely to be permanently disabled or to suffer a critical illness than he is to die within the next 20 years. So if the arguments to support buying life insurance are convincing, the arguments in favour of an income replacement policy are perhaps even more compelling.

Despite all these figures, this sort of protection is taken out by very few people – an estimated 15% of the working population. There are a number of reasons for this, not least the name under which income replacement cover had traditionally been marketed: 'permanent health insurance', or simply PHI. It is easy to see why many potential buyers would be put off by a name like this, and why others would assume it had something to do with paying medical expenses rather than replacing income.

Just to reiterate, then: permanent health insurance is better described as income replacement insurance (something the insurers have at last cottoned onto); and income replacement insurance pays a regular income, which has been agreed in advance, to the policyholder when he or she is unable to work because of illness or disablement.

State Provision*

* All figures for State benefits are correct from April 1996.

People do not insure their incomes in this way because they assume that, if they are off work through illness, the Government or their employer will somehow take care of them. Sadly, this is far from being the case. All employers have to pay Statutory Sick Pay of at least £54.55 per week. Enlightened employers will often top this up, especially in the case of valued staff, but even the most generous firm will impose a time-limit of some kind. This is quite understandable: just consider the cost of paying a non-productive person's salary for years or even decades.

State benefits, meanwhile, will not keep you in anything like the style to which you've become accustomed as a salaried employee. In 1995 a new class of payment, Incapacity Benefit, replaced the old invalidity and sickness benefits. Incapacity benefit is paid after the first 28 weeks of sickness, during which time most people will receive their Statutory Sick Pay (SSP). Those unable to get SSP – mainly those who are self-employed – are entitled to a lower rate of Incapacity Benefit straightaway (£46.15 a week). Benefit paid after 28 weeks is taxable.

Incapacity Benefit is termed a 'contributory' benefit, which means that only those who have paid sufficient National Insurance Contributions (NICs) are entitled to it. Others will have to apply for Income Support, which is means-tested. In other words, if you have other sources of income (perhaps from your investments), substantial capital savings or a working partner, you may not qualify for assistance until the bulk of your own resources has been used up.

Another change introduced in 1995 is intended to reduce the number of people qualifying for Incapacity Benefit. Under the old regime, benefits were paid to those judged unfit to do their own job. Under the new regime, incapacity benefit is only paid to those who are assessed as being unfit to do *any* job. This makes it more likely that skilled and experienced employees will be refused benefit because, although they cannot return to their old job, they could retrain to carry out other work. So high-powered executives might have their applications turned down because they are fit enough to work as car-park attendants. It sounds extreme, but it has happened.

Yet another change concerns the state of the sick or injured person's health. Judgements about claimants' fitness for work used to be made by their own doctor; now they are made by independent assessors. Critics of this development suggest that, given the tenor of the other changes, which are designed to cut State spending on benefits, people will be receiving a less sympathetic hearing because the independent assessors will be much less willing to write a sick note than family GPs.

Those who are judged capable of working but who are unable to find a job can claim Unemployment Benefit, which is payable for 12 months to those with sufficient NICs. From April 1996 this benefit will be replaced by the Job-Seeker's Allowance, which will be paid for only six months before a means test is imposed.

These changes not only affect general eligibility for State assistance in the event of illness, but also the amount that is paid to those whose claim is successful. The low level of benefit has always made income replacement insurance a good idea; the 1995 changes have virtually made it a necessity if financial hardship is to be avoided.

Before the changes took effect an individual claimant received a weekly £57.60 Invalidity Benefit after 28 weeks off work. Now, the individual short-term Incapacity Benefit, which is payable from weeks 28 to 52, is £54.55. The old earnings-related supplement has disappeared and, as Table 8 shows, allowances for dependants have also fallen. You can claim £28.55 for a dependant adult, £9.90 for the eldest child and £11.15 for each other child. (It is interesting to speculate how these figures are reached. Why not round the figures up to £10 for the first child and down to £11 for the rest? Wouldn't that make things that little bit simpler?)

Long-term incapacity benefit, meanwhile, which kicks in after 53 weeks, is payable at a basic rate of £61.15, with the same additional benefits available for dependant children. There is a benefit of £36.60 for a dependant adult, but this is only payable if he or she is caring for children or is over 60. These are hardly princely sums and, as suggested earlier, anyone used to a regular wage or salary cheque will very quickly feel the pinch.

How Does Income Replacement Cover Work?

An income replacement policy pays a regular income while you are unable to work because of illness or the effect of an accident on your health. The payments continue until you are fit enough to return to work or until you reach retirement age, whichever comes first. The payments are normally made monthly.

Some employers offer income replacement protection as a perk (on which you have to pay tax), but this is not nearly as widespread a benefit as private medical insurance. For most of us, therefore, the answer is an individual policy – a basic insurance contract between the policyholder and the insurance company. It is possible to buy this sort of cover through an insurance broker or direct from the company itself.

Table 8: How the changes to sickness benefits have affected claims

Example (a)
A married man aged 45 earning £26,000 per annum with two dependant children.

Old entitlement after 28 weeks		*New entitlement from weeks 28–52*
£57.60	Individual claimant	£54.55
£34.50	Adult dependant	£28.55
£9.80	First dependant child	£9.90
£11.15	Second dependant child	£11.15
£63.70	Earnings related supplement	—
£176.60	TOTAL	£104.15

Percentage reduction in benefit received: 41%

Example (b)
A married couple with one earner aged 55 earning £15,600 per annum, and two children aged 19 and 20.

Old entitlement after 28 weeks		*New entitlement from weeks 28–52*
£57.60	Individual claimant	£54.55
£34.50	Adult dependant	—
£42.70	Earnings related supplement	—
£134.80	TOTAL	£54.55

Percentage reduction in benefit received: 60%

Source: Medical Sickness Society

Income replacement cover is what is known as a long-term contract, rather than an annual policy like motor or household insurance. This means there is no renewal date; you just keep paying premiums and, as long as you do so, the insurance company is obliged to honour your claims, regardless of how many you make. For this reason, you have to continue paying premiums even when you are making a claim, although many policies for an additional premium offer an option that waives payment of premiums while benefits are being paid.

Income replacement insurance premiums increase throughout the life of the policy to reflect the insurance company's rising costs. It is possible, however, to obtain 'guaranteed' premiums from a number of companies, whereby premiums will not be increased by more than the rate of inflation. Ask the insurance company about its attitude to guarantees or discuss the matter with your broker.

This type of insurance pays out when you are off work. If you are able to return to a lower-paid job than your original occupation, your policy might make up the shortfall in your earnings. Again, this is something you should discuss before you commit to a contract.

Benefit limits

There is a limit on how much benefit can be paid by an income replacement scheme. In short, when you add any State benefits to your insurance payments, you will not receive more than 75% of the money you were earning before you were forced to stop work. The logic here is obvious: if it were possible to be as well off when claiming benefits as when working, it seems many of us would take the opportunity to stay at home. The limit therefore discourages malingerers.

Even with the 75% ceiling in place, insurance companies are always aware that some might find it attractive to receive benefits instead of work. Accordingly, they employ inspectors to check on the progress of their policyholders – and to make sure that those who are fit do not continue to receive payments.

Tax

From 6 April 1996, benefits are not subject to tax for as long as the claimant is sick or disabled. Previously, benefits paid by income replacement schemes were normally subject to tax once they had been paid for the full 12 months from 6 April in one year through to 5 April in the next (a full 'fiscal' year). The new rules mean income replacement cover is now better value for money when claims last for the appropriate length of time. However, when the benefits are provided via an employer's scheme they are taxed immediately.

How Much Does Income Replacement Cover Cost?

The cost of income replacement, like the cost of many forms of insurance, is determined by a number of factors, including your age, health, whether or not you smoke and your occupation. For example, older people can expect to pay more as they are at greater risk of becoming seriously ill and disabled. Again, if you have pre-existing medical conditions, they will usually be excluded from the scope of the policy; if your general state of health is poor, you will have to pay more.

Sex
The sex of the policyholder is taken into account when calculating the premiums. With term insurance, women pay less because, on average, they live longer. With income replacement cover, however, women tend to pay more because, statistically, they are more susceptible to illness and more likely to be off work as a result.

A number of women have tried to challenge the basis on which insurers make their calculations, claiming that their premiums were unfairly high. They contend that the statistics are skewed because they do not recognize that many women take days off work not because of their own illness but in order to look after sick children – or even sick male partners – whereas men largely do not share this type of responsibility. Such absences from work are generally for short periods and should therefore not be taken into account when calculating the risk of long-term incapacity. Insurers have been taken to court by women anxious to press this case, but the discrepancies between male and female premium rates remain.

Occupation
Those in dangerous jobs where the risk of accident or injury is higher will also have to stump up for bigger premiums. As a

general rule, those in sedentary and clerical occupations will pay less than those with manual jobs. This means that, if you change job, your cover may be invalidated. Alternatively, the insurance company may simply adjust the premium to reflect the new risk that you present.

It is essential that you tell the insurer as soon as any such change takes place. Do not assume that your cover is still valid, or you may end up with nothing when you claim.

Amount of benefit

Other factors that will affect the cost of income replacement cover include the number of dependants you have, the amount of benefit you require – obviously the size of the premium is linked to the size of the potential payout – and the 'deferred period'.

When working how much benefit you want to receive if you are unable to earn, there is no point picking a figure that bears no relation to your salary. Too high, and you will run up against the 75% rule; too low, and the money you save on your premiums will soon be swallowed up as you struggle to make ends meet.

To calculate the correct level of benefit, write down your regular monthly commitments, including an amount for spending on clothes and holidays and other occasional expenses. Remember that, if you have a company car, it will probably have to go back to the pool if you are not working, so travelling expenses must come into your calculations. But remember that in some areas you will be spending less: if you normally commute to work and buy expensive sandwiches for lunch every day, you should make the appropriate deductions from the required amount of benefit. You will probably also find that, if you are ill or injured, your monthly expenditure on entertainment will fall. Most people elect for a benefit level somewhere between half and three-quarters of their take-home pay.

Deferred period

The deferred period is the length of time after you become ill before the income replacement benefit is payable. You may

Table 9: The cost of PHI

Example (a)

The monthly cost for income replacement insurance for a variety of individuals, all of whom are non-smokers in low risk occupations and in good health. In each case benefit is index-linked and is deferred for 13 weeks (one of the most popular waiting times).

	Benefit (paid until)	Allied Dunbar	Friends Provident	Norwich Union	UNUM
Male, 35	£500 (65)	£17.90	£19.22*	£14.50	£14.65
Female, 35	£500 (65)**	£30.74	£27.38*	£20.25	£20.95
Male, 45	£750 (65)	£48.05	£36.91*	£34.43	£35.97
Female, 50	£1,000 (60)	£86.30	£60.73*	£57.30	£67.20

* Friends Provident premiums increase at the rate of 5% per annum compound throughout the term of the policy because the policy is index-linked.

** Maximum plan termination age for women is 60.

Example (b)

The monthly premium costs for annual benefit of £17,000, payable to retirement at 65 (assuming male aged 40 in low risk clerical employment).

Insurer	Type of benefit	Monthly premium Deferment		
		3 months	*6 months*	*12 months*
Allied Dunbar	Level	£39.50	£25.90	£23.86
	Index-linked	£63.47	£34.06	£30.49
Friends Provident	Level	£52.38	£43.88	£37.34
	Increasing cover*	£56.63	£55.65	£44.86
Norwich Union	Index-linked	£46.22	£30.21	£26.24
UNUM	Level	£35.87	£29.33	£23.08
	Index-linked	£48.66	£39.74	£30.66

* The increasing cover benefit increases at 5% per annum.

choose a number of weeks (the minimum is normally four) to six months, a year or even two years. The longer the deferred period, the lower the premium.

When choosing your deferred period – perhaps better referred to as 'waiting time' – you should certainly calculate how much premium you can afford, but you should also consider how much of your savings you want to dip into before the policy begins to pay out. If you have plenty of capital, you might be prepared to wait some time; if your savings are almost non-existent, you might be willing to pay a higher premium in order to receive benefit sooner.

You should also check your employer's attitude to Non-statutory Sick Pay. If you are lucky enough to work for a firm that will pay a decent proportion of your salary for a reasonable period, you might feel able to choose a longer deferred period and save on premiums.

Index-linking

Most income replacement insurers offer an option to index-link the benefit, which means that, for an additional premium, the benefits will rise in line with inflation. This is an invaluable feature for those who face the prospect of being off work for any length of time.

Guaranteed premiums

If you are offered 'guaranteed premiums', the insurance company is promising not to increase premiums by anything more than the rate of inflation during the life of the policy. Otherwise you risk a hefty premium increase if the company suffers a lot of claims.

6 || *Mortgage Payment Protection Insurance*

Mortgage payment protection insurance (MPPI) offers specific cover for what is likely to be your biggest single item of expenditure. It pays out not only if you are unable to earn a living due to illness or injury; it also covers you if you are made redundant. This insurance safety-net can be very comforting if you are concerned about job security in these times of economic uncertainty.

As you might expect, MPPI is mainly sold by mortgage lenders. (In some cases, if you are taking out a special fixed-rate mortgage deal, for example, you may find that this cover is compulsory.) But two big insurance companies – General Accident and Sun Alliance – recently opened up the market to a greater degree of competition when they started selling cover direct to the public. You can also buy a policy through your mortgage broker or insurance adviser.

In the past cover was generally only made available to people at the time they actually took out their mortgage, but the arrival of new sales methods, coupled with changes to the rules governing State support for borrowers who become unemployed, mean existing borrowers are now being offered cover as well.

The changes to the Income Support rules were one of the most controversial measures introduced by the Government in 1995. Prior to 1 October borrowers who lost their income because of unemployment or disability were able to apply for Income Support. This paid 50% of the interest on their loan for the first 16 weeks of a claim. After 16 weeks the full amount of interest was paid. Since 1 October those who already have mortgages and who make a claim for benefit receive no payment for two months and then receive

50% of the interest for the following four months. Full interest payments are made after six months. Those who have taken out their mortgage since 1 October 1995 and who have subsequently become eligible for Income Support receive nothing towards the cost of mortgage interest for the first nine months of the claim.

Remember that Income Support is means-tested. Anyone with savings, a working spouse or partner or another source of income – from an investment portfolio, for example – is unlikely to qualify. Savings of £3,000 will begin to erode entitlement; £8,000 will remove entitlement altogether. It is estimated that 70% of borrowers would not qualify for the benefit for one reason or another.

Income Support only pays mortgage *interest*. It makes no contribution towards repayment of the capital debt or to any investment policy that is being funded to repay an interest-only loan. And bear in mind that Income Support will only pay the interest on the first £100,000 of any mortgage. In other words, if you have a £150,000 mortgage, you will get no help whatsoever on the interest that is due on £50,000 of the loan.

The Government's clear intention has been to relieve the burden on the State by forcing borrowers to make private provision in the form of MPPI.

How Does MPPI Work?

Wherever you buy cover – from your lender, direct from an insurance company or through a broker – the policy will work in much the same way. You pay a premium each month and if you become unemployed or unable to work because of an accident or sickness, the policy will pay your mortgage for you. As you would expect, however, this simple concept has the usual baggage of conditions and exceptions.

Who can buy MPPI?
Cover is generally available to mortgage borrowers aged between 18 and 60. They must have been in continuous employment for a

certain length of time – some insurers stipulate six months, some a year – and they must work a minimum number of hours – usually 16 – each week. They must not be aware of any impending cause of unemployment and they must be in good health.

Length of payment period

Payments will normally be made until you find work or for 12 months, whichever period is shorter. Some policies stretch the payments to 24 months, while others cover claims for unemployment for 12 months and claims for other reasons for longer. According to insurance company statistics, the average length of a claim is five to six months.

Qualifying periods

MPPI insurers are extremely wary of people taking out cover knowing that they are about to lose their job, so policies come with a 'qualifying period' – the length of time that a policy must be in force before a claim will be accepted. This period varies from policy to policy and may be as short as 60 days or as long as 180.

Again, some policies make a distinction between unemployment and disability: the qualifying period may apply for claims following redundancy but not for those caused by accident or sickness.

Waiting times

All MPPI policies require a period of time to elapse before benefits will be paid. This is sometimes referred to as the 'excess' period and lasts for between 30 and 90 days. Insurers say they require this waiting period because some people find a new job within a relatively short period of time anyway, but in practice the excess is a way of reducing the number of claims and therefore keeping premiums affordable.

The amount of cover

When you buy MPPI, you need to decide how much monthly benefit you would need to cover your actual mortgage payments and any other related outgoings, such as household insurance and contributions towards an investment policy. However, limits will be imposed on the amount of cover you can buy: the minimum is generally £100, with maximum amounts ranging from £1,000 to £1,500 per month. Additionally, the maximum amount will vary depending on individual circumstances and will be expressed as a percentage – typically 120% or 125% – of your total mortgage commitments each month.

Self-employed borrowers

Many policies specifically exclude the self-employed. This is because insurers fear that it will be difficult to prove that the policyholder is genuinely unemployed rather than lazy. Some of those policies that do offer cover to the self-employed require the individual to be registered bankrupt before paying a claim.

More enlightened insurers have recognized that an increasing number of people are working for themselves and have therefore included the appropriate cover in their policies. However, self-employed policyholders will still have to demonstrate that their business has ceased to be viable and that the downturn is not simply due to factors that are seasonal or otherwise predictable and commonplace in their line of work.

Those working on fixed-term contracts may also find it difficult to obtain unemployment (but not accident and sickness) cover, although some policies cover redundancy if the contract is cancelled mid-term. Employment by renewable contract is becoming increasingly common in a number of industries and the most advanced policies will treat policyholders in the same way as normal employees if their contract is renewed a certain number of times (normally three).

Unemployment

As you might expect, MPPI policies will not pay out for unemployment if the policyholder becomes voluntarily unemployed or is dismissed as a result of misconduct. Unemployment as a result of industrial action is also not covered.

Joint mortgages

MPPI policies recognize the fact that many modern mortgages are arranged in joint names, with each partner contributing towards the cost. Where this is the case, and if both partners meet the application requirements, they can both have cover.

The normal practice is for the monthly benefit to be split according to the proportion of the total income earned by each partner. Thus, if a wife earns £300 per month and her husband earns £200, 60% of the benefit will be paid if she claims and 40% will be paid if he claims.

Moving house

MPPI cover is normally invalidated when you move house, so a new policy will be required. If you stay with the same insurer, you will probably have to go through the qualifying period for a second time; this is always the case if you go to a new company. Again, as this type of insurance develops, we may see the introduction of policies that allow a smoother transfer from one property to another.

Making a Claim

As with any type of insurance, you should tell the insurance company as soon as possible if you expect to make a claim. The insurer will ask you to complete a claims form and supply evidence in support of your claim. In case of sickness or accident you will have to show that you have been signed off work by a doctor. If you become unemployed, you will need to show your redundancy notice and to register with the Employment Service as someone who is actively seeking work.

How Much Does MPPI Cost?

MPPI policies are usually sold on a fixed-rate basis, which means that if your application is accepted, you pay the going rate charged by that particular provider. In other words, the premiums do not vary from individual to individual according to their particular details.

That said, however, General Accident's latest policy, which is available over the telephone, charges premiums that reflect the risk profile of each applicant. If demand for MPPI picks up following the changes in the Income Support rules, more insurance companies may decide to adopt this approach. As with other forms of insurance sold over the telephone, the GA product is cheaper than many policies sold by traditional methods, with premiums ranging from £4 to £5 per month for every £100 of cover required, compared to the usual £5 to £7 per month for each £100.

This area of the insurance market is likely to see continued change as lenders, borrowers and insurers adjust to the tough Income Support regime. Already one lender, Skipton Building Society, has stirred things up by offering free unemployment cover to both existing and new borrowers. It has also cut premium rates for accident and sickness protection, with cover available at £4.50 a month per £100 of cover.

As a form of 'general' insurance, your MPPI cover will attract insurance premium tax at 2.5% of the premium.

When looking for cover, remember that policies are available from a variety of sources, so if you are not happy with the insurance provided by your lender, by all means shop around. However, if you have a mortgage with one lender, you cannot get MPPI from another lender; you will have to go direct to an insurance company or consult a broker.

7 ‖ *Long-term Care Insurance*

Thinking about your insurance needs inevitably means confronting taboo subjects that we normally try to avoid thinking about – death, of course, but also the prospect of being ill, injured or unemployed and, most difficult to face of all, perhaps, old age. If we remain hale and hearty and enjoy our retirement years in good health, all well and good. But what if we fall ill? Who will look after us? Will we become a burden to our family, or be shunted off to end our days in some grim nursing home? Will our life's savings be eaten up with the cost of accommodation and nursing care, leaving nothing to be passed on to our children?

The State and Care of the Elderly

Too many people try to brush these questions under the carpet by telling themselves that the State will look after them. But look at the mounting demands on the State's resources – the Department of Social Security swallows a massive £80 billion budget every year and still struggles to fulfil its obligations – you will see that the State simply cannot be expected to take care of us. And if the situation is desperate now, what will things be like when we are old and need assistance?

More people are living longer, which means that those in work are having to support an ever-growing number of pensioners. In a political climate where tax increases are a sensitive issue for all parties, the emphasis is moving away from State to private provision. This is not only the case with pensions but with all the other facilities that were once automatically provided by the authorities.

The Development of LTC

As we, as a nation, grow older, more of us need medical attention. Medicine may have been able to increase our life expectancy, but it has yet to find a cure for the problems associated with old age. This has led to the development in recent years of long-term care (LTC) insurance, which is designed to pay for nursing help at home or for a residential or nursing home.

When you buy LTC you are planning for the future and, as with most sorts of financial planning, the earlier you start the better. It is reckoned that the best time to buy LTC is between the age of 60 and 65, which will usually give you plenty of time before you are likely to make a claim, thereby reducing the size of the premium. The later you buy, the sooner the possible claim and the greater the cost. Eventually you will not be able to buy cover at all. Insurers impose an upper age limit (normally 80 or 85) beyond which they will not issue a policy since the likelihood of an early claim is so much greater. Moreover, the cost of LTC is also determined in part by your state of health, so it makes sense to buy earlier rather than wait for the onset of illness to act as a trigger for a distress purchase.

Insurance companies are sometimes unable to resist the temptation to bombard us with all manner of frightening statistics in order to persuade us to buy a policy, but these scaremongering tactics canot disguise the fact that the figures are genuinely alarming.

Living longer

In 1990 20.8% of the UK population was aged 60 or over; by 2030 this figure will be almost 30%. You may think 2030 is a long way off, but remember that those who are in their late 20s in 1996 will have reached that age by then.

Life expectancy has been improving steadily as medical skills have developed. At the beginning of this century a newborn baby boy had a life expectancy of just under 46 years. In 1992 a boy could look forward to nearly 74 years and women live longer by an average of five years. Reductions in infant mortality have contributed largely to this improvement, but better diet, healthier lifestyles and superior medical care are constantly pushing back the average date of death. In 1901 a 60-year-old man could have expected to live another 13 years or so. In 1992 he might feel aggrieved if he didn't get another 18 years, and by the year 2021 he will be justified in looking forward to his 81st birthday.

By the year 2000 there will be 1.2 million pensioners over the grand old age of 85 – 2% of the population; but by the year 2050 the figure will be over 3 million, which will be 5% of the population, or one person in 20. The distant future? Hello again to our friends in their 20s.

Health in old age
Over half of those aged 65 or over suffer from a disabling disease and a quarter are confined to their homes. Over 550,000 people are in full-time nursing and residential care facilities, and if this population continues to grow at the present rate, a further 70,000 places will be needed by the end of the century. By the year 2050 1.3 million such places will be required.

The cost of care
Staying in a nursing home costs a lot of money. The actual figures depend on the quality of the accommodation and the level of care required, but a typical nursing home might charge £350 per week, with residential accommodation costing around £250 per week. Think of this in terms of nearly £18,000 a year for nursing care and you get some idea of the sums involved.

Meeting these costs is not a matter for the NHS, which is concerned with aiding short-term, acute conditions rather than providing care on a long-term basis. Since the Community Care Act of 1993, responsibility for the provision of State care to the elderly has rested with local authorities.

Who bears the cost?

Assistance for those needing care in old age is means tested. In other words, if you have the means to pay, then pay you must. Actual practice varies from one local authority to another, but the basic rule is that your costs will only be met if you have less than £10,000 of capital; if you have more than £16,000 of capital, no assistance whatsoever will be provided by the local authority. If you have capital between these figures, you will receive a contribution towards your expenses.

Some authorities define 'capital' as savings and investments and will simply require a declaration of how much money is held in bank and building society accounts or in things such as Peps, TESSAs and other financial products. Others, however, will include everything within the definition of capital, including a person's house. Homeowners are therefore unlikely to receive a contribution from their local authority.

Obviously, if you are living at home while receiving nursing care, it may not be practicable to sell the property. But authorities may charge against your property and reclaim the outstanding costs of any care they have funded when the property is eventually sold.

The Insurance Solution

Long-term care (LTC) insurance pays towards the costs you might incur in old age, such as nursing care at home, additional help around the home or residential and nursing home care. It is different from medical insurance, which pays for treatment of acute, normally short-term conditions. LTC, on the other hand, acknowledges that the problem is a long-term one that is unlikely to improve.

Most policies fix an agreed amount of benefit to be paid each week. If your care actually costs less, the lesser amount will be paid. A basic contract will cover nursing in your own home or in an approved nursing home, while more expensive policies will also pay for someone to do the housekeeping. Deluxe contracts will provide what is known as 'respite' care. This is payment for occasional professional help to give family members or other people taking care of you a break from their daily duties. A top-of-the-range policy will also pay for improvements to be made to your home, such as the installation of lifts, ramps and other measures to help you get about more easily. Policies may also pay for medical services such as chiropody, physiotherapy, speech and occupational therapy.

Countering inflation

One of the prime causes of price inflation in any sphere is demand. As we have seen, the demand for nursing and residential care is growing and will continue to grow. This means that prices will continue to rise, so it makes sense to link benefits payable under LTC insurance to increases in costs – a process referred to as 'index-linking'. In this way, the benefits anticipate what the actual costs might be a few years hence when a claim is made.

How much cover should you buy?

When you discuss LTC with a broker or an insurance company, you should receive from them details of how much nursing care or residential accommodation costs in your area (there can be marked differences according to where you live). This will give you some idea of what sort of benefit level to select. You may not automatically want to go into residential accommodation in the area where you live at the moment. Perhaps you want to be closer to your family or simply to be in the country or near the sea. If this is the case, ask for details of prices in that area as well.

Some policies are simply designed to pay in benefit whatever the cost of care turns out to be. This may sound ideal, but it is usually more expensive; you may have other sources of income, such as State and other pensions, interest on savings and dividends on investments. If you are living in a residential home or confined to your own home, you may not have much opportunity to spend this money, in which case it would be better to use the LTC benefit to top-up existing income. Obviously, the lower the benefit level selected, the cheaper the premiums.

Couples
LTC is expensive, so insuring two people will be doubly so. It is generally concluded that, in the case of a couple, it is best to assume that one partner will look after the other for as long as is necessary. Cover is therefore normally arranged for whichever survives the other.

Funding for a lifetime's care
There are two basic types of policy. With the first, you invest a lump sum into an investment fund and create what might be termed your long-term care kitty. This is looked after for you by the insurance company until you make a claim, when it is used to pay benefits. The obvious danger with this type of policy is that the kitty will be exhausted if you survive for a long time. You would then be at the mercy of local authority means testing and possibly be forced to use your private savings to pay for your care.

The second type of policy entitles you to benefits that will be paid for life. You can buy this sort of policy either with a lump sum or with regular premium contributions. Insurance companies know that some people may claim the day after they take out their policy and receive benefits for many years, but they also know that others will have their policy for many years and perhaps never make a claim, so there is a balancing-out of costs.

When you pay regular premiums, they do not increase with age like many medical insurance policies. However, the insurance company will reserve the right to review premiums if it suddenly finds itself paying out on a lot of claims and running short of money as a result. That said, many policies come with a guarantee that premiums will not be increased for a certain length of time – five or 10 years, for example.

Following the 1995 Budget, consultations are taking place

between the Government and insurance companies on new ways of funding LTC policies. Specifically, attention is being given to 'partnership' schemes, where those who effect certain levels of insurance will receive extra State help, and links to pension funds, where accumulated investments could be released gradually to pay premiums.

When does a claim become payable?

Insurance companies judge whether a claim should be paid according to the policyholders' ability to carry out certain 'activities of daily living' (ADLs) – typically, these six:

- General mobility (measured by the ability to get out of bed and into a chair)
- Dressing
- Eating
- Bathing
- Using the lavatory
- Walking.

If you cannot manage a certain number of these tasks, then benefits will be paid for the appropriate level of care. Payment will also be made if the care is deemed necessary by a doctor. Some insurers impose more stringent ADL tests than others, and some require an inability to perform three while others settle for only two. This is one of the factors to be taken into account when choosing a policy.

Insurers also measure what is known as cognitive ability, which may be affected by ailments such as Alzheimer's Disease and other conditions leading to the onset of senility. Different companies have different ideas on what constitutes cognitive impairment, but a claim will normally be paid when it is agreed that it is no longer safe or practical for you to continue living in your own home.

How much does LTC cost?

Unlike medical insurance for the elderly, there is no tax relief on LTC premiums: they are invested in special tax-exempt funds, which means the insurance company does not have to pay tax on any profits it makes within the fund. Also, the benefits will be paid tax-free.

Benefits from a policy will either be paid directly to the organization that is providing the care or to the policyholder to pay for visiting carers who help in the policyholder's home.

To maximize the tax efficiency of buying LTC, some companies suggest that it is bought with the tax-free cash available from a pension fund on retirement.

The need for advice
With such a sensitive topic as long-term care, it is important to involve relations and friends and to get expert advice and assistance. For example, it might make sense to redistribute assets to other members of your family so that you will be more likely to qualify for local authority assistance. All manner of complicated tax problems arise with gifts of this sort, so make sure you get professional help to avoid or at least reduce your potential liability to Inheritance Tax. Skilled guidance might even be useful when applying for State assistance – a daunting prospect for some.

When you take a look at your situation in old age, you may also start thinking about other related matters, such as how to settle your affairs and who might control them in the event of dementia. These are all nettles that are best grasped lest they grow and blight your prospects of a happy retirement.

Table 10: Sample costs of long-term care insurance

This table details monthly premiums for individuals of various ages requiring a benefit of £1,000 per month. Benefits are index-linked and will rise by up to 5% per annum.

Age of applicant	Male	Female
60	£52.87	£62.06
65	£71.26	£80.46
70	£93.10	£101.15
75	£111.49	£159.77

Source: PPP Lifetime

8 | *Critical Illness Insurance*

Cancer . . . heart attack . . . stroke . . . these are words that strike fear into us all – and with good reason, for they are alarmingly common. Each year over 300,000 people in the UK are diagnosed as having some form of cancer; over 150,000 suffer a heart attack and 100,000 a stroke. These are just three of the so-called 'critical' illnesses. In all, 20% of the UK population will be struck down by a serious ailment of one sort or another before they reach 65.

Confronting issues like serious illness is difficult, not least because it raises the ultimate taboo subject: death. But thanks to advances in medical science, the problem faced by people who contract such an illness is often not death, but life. In other words, the care and attention they receive can help them to survive, but they will suddenly have to adapt to a totally new set of circumstances. Again, the statistics are telling: one person in every three will develop cancer at some point, but of those who contract the disease, one in three will survive for three years or more. As for heart attacks, of those 150,000 who suffer each year, well over half will still be alive a year later; nearly 80,000 of the 100,000 stroke victims will survive for at least a year.

Needless to say, there are financial implications to surviving the onset of a critical illness, so insurance companies now offer critical illness insurance. This type of protection pays out a lump sum when one of a range of specified illnesses is diagnosed or following serious injury in an accident – money that can come in useful in a wide range of circumstances. Those in work, for example, will probably find that they have to give up their job for a considerable length of time while they convalesce. They might even have to give up work altogether, or perhaps find another job which is less strenuous or stressful – and perhaps less lucrative.

Those in paid employment are not the only ones who need be concerned about their situation. Those who look after the home and children face enormous demands in terms of time and energy – demands which simply could not be met during a period of convalescence. Partners, friends, and family might rally round to help, but it is highly unlikely that they would be able to take on all the chores, which means hiring someone to help out – not a cheap option.

There will probably be other costs to worry about (just when your doctor tells you to try not to worry about anything): as you recover from your illness, you might need nursing care and other professional services; you might have to make alterations to your house in order to allow wheelchair access; a downstairs bathroom or a chair-lift might be essential. You might also be told to rest and take an extended holiday – a great idea, but also a potentially expensive one. Where would the money come from? If you dipped into your savings for this or for any of the other costs, how, financially, would this affect the rest of your life? And not just for *your* life: what about your partner and your children? All your dreams and ambitions might be destroyed as you struggle to cope with your predicament.

Some of the costs following the onset of a critical illness might be met by other insurance arrangements. For instance, medical insurance might pay for private treatment, while income protection cover would help compensate for lost earnings. If you are blessed with a particularly progressive employer, you may find that your salary continues to be paid while you recover. You would also be entitled to certain State benefits and, of course, you would be entitled to a great deal of medical treatment free under the National Health Service.

But even if the bulk of your medical bills are taken care of, and even if your income remains relatively intact, you could still find life a struggle. The lump sum benefit from a critical illness contract gives you incalculable peace of mind because it allows you and your family to take the sort of action necessary for your recovery and comfort without having to worry about cost. Only with a sizeable sum of money in the bank will you be able to contemplate recuperative holidays, home improvements and adaptations or moving house.

How Does Critical Illness Cover Work?

Critical illness insurance is available in a variety of forms, either as a 'stand-alone' policy or as part of another protection contract. If you are interested in buying cover, you should take into account your existing policies and your financial obligations to help you decide which policy is best for you.

Fixed term cover

As its name suggests, this sort of policy provides protection for a certain length of time or up to a certain age, such as 60 or 65. This might suit someone who has an outstanding debt (such as a mortgage) and who wishes to arrange for it to be repaid should they suffer a critical illness. In this regard, the policy is similar to the straightforward term assurance mentioned in Chapter 1 (see page 7), which pays out a lump sum in the event of death. Someone with a mortgage might therefore match their critical illness protection to their outstanding liability so that they will not have to find the mortgage repayments every month if they become critically ill.

You are covered only up to a certain age – usually retirement age – because, once you receive a pension, you will no longer have the same worries about losing your only source of income because of incapacity. By the time you retire you are unlikely to be financially responsible for your children, so there would be one less drain on your resources. Moreover, when you stop work, you may no longer be able to afford the premiums.

This term cover option is also the cheapest, since the insurance company knows that the risk of your falling victim to a critical condition before retirement age is lower.

Lifetime cover

At whatever stage in your life you contract a critical illness or suffer the consequences of an accident, you could benefit from receiving a cash lump sum, so this sort of policy remains in effect until you die. Needless to say, premiums have to be paid for longer and are also more expensive because of the greater risk of a claim being made.

As with whole of life insurance (see page 14), which pays out whenever you die, the premiums for this sort of critical illness cover are sometimes only payable up to a certain age, such as 75 or 80. The price paid throughout the time the premiums are payable reflects the fact that cover continues after they have stopped.

Some insurance companies offer policies that combine life assurance and critical illness protection, and here you may come across the phrase 'accelerated death benefit'. This is yet another of those confusing technical terms favoured by the insurance industry; it simply means that the sum assured – normally payable on death – will be paid in the event of a critical illness being diagnosed.

Mortgage plans

Many endowment policies come with an option to take out critical illness cover, which means that the borrower's outstanding debt will be settled in the case of diagnosis of illness.

Protecting your family

Critical illness policies can be bought by individuals (known as 'single life basis') or by couples ('joint life basis'). In the latter case, the policy will pay out when either partner is diagnosed as having a critical illness, thus helping the other to cope with the inevitable shock and upheaval.

It is also possible to buy policies that include children's cover. This provides for a certain cash sum (which may be a fixed amount, such as £10,000, or a percentage of the main sum assured) to be paid out if the child is diagnosed as having a specified illness. The intention here is to provide the parents with a financial cushion to help them look after the child, freeing them from the anxieties that might otherwise be caused by having to take time off work. It should be noted, however, that the list of ailments covered by the children's section of the policy will not be as extensive as for the adults.

What is covered by critical illness insurance?
Critical illness insurance is a relatively new concept in the UK – the first policies were sold as recently as 1986. Lots of companies now offer the product, but there are still marked differences in approach – not every ailment is covered by every policy, for example – so always check the extent of cover. Having said that, a number of core conditions are common to virtually all policies. These are:

- Heart attack
- Cancer
- Stroke
- Kidney failure
- Coronary artery bypass
- Major organ transplants.

While the latter two in this list may not be strictly defined as illnesses, they lead to the same sort of problems and are therefore covered.

Depending on how comprehensive the cover offered by the policy, additional illnesses may also be included, for example:

- Paralysis
- Loss of limbs, sight, hearing or speech
- Severe burns

- Coma
- Multiple sclerosis
- Alzheimer's disease
- Parkinson's disease
- Motor neurone disease.

Some insurers add further diseases and conditions, with some offering protection on as many as 30 separate illnesses. Others refrain from explicitly naming the conditions and instead offer a looser definition of incapacity or reduced ability to carry out a normal life, thus embracing a wide range of problems without having to list every possibility. One such catch-all definition is 'total and permanent disability', often abbreviated to TPD. This is the same sort of cover included in income replacement schemes: the benefit will be paid if the policyholder is rendered unable to continue working.

Some insurers will only pay benefits when policyholders are unable to carry out *any* occupation. In other words, if they are able to do a job other than their own, they will not get paid. Others pay benefits as soon as they are unable to do their own job. The latter type will be more expensive. Given that this element of the critical illness policy is work-related, it will normally only last until retirement age; other insured conditions which result in TPD, such as loss of limbs, may still trigger a claim at a later stage.

Another cover-all concerns what is termed 'irreversible disability' – sometimes described as the inability to continue normal life, or the loss of independent existence. This covers some of the debilitating and degenerative diseases listed above (such as Parkinson's and Alzheimer's). You qualify for benefit under this section of a policy if you are unable to perform two or perhaps three of the 'activities of daily living' already mentioned in the previous chapter – namely:

- General mobility (measured by the ability to get out of bed and into a chair)

- Dressing
- Eating
- Bathing
- Using the lavatory
- Walking.

When choosing between policies, always check whether conditions that might lead to irreversible disability are also covered in their own right. One policy will not necessarily offer more cover than another, but if the disease is listed separately, payment will be made when the illness is diagnosed, rather than when it leads to irreversible disability. This distinction appears a subtle one, but it can make a substantial difference to the quality of life of the policyholder and his or her family.

A third cover-all definition will ensure that benefit is paid on diagnosis of any terminal illness. There are different definitions in force depending on which policy you buy. For example, some define a terminal illness as one which will lead to death within 12 months; others allow a longer period between diagnosis and death. Some policies include AIDS and related conditions within their definition, while others exclude them altogether.

How Much Does Critical Illness Cover Cost?

The cost of cover is determined by a number of factors, including age, health, sex and the amount of cover required. Different premiums will also be charged depending on whether or not you smoke. If you opt for a high sum assured, above £250,000 or £500,000, say, you will be required to undergo a medical examination. The average sum assured for policies currently in force is little under £50,000. Benefits are tax-free.

Table 11: Critical illness insurance – typical monthly premiums

Example (a)
Non-smokers. Sum assured: £50,000

Age next birthday	Length of term (years)	Males	Females
30	10	£10.90	£12.70
40	10	£22.25	£20.40
50	10	£48.60	£39.85
30	15	£11.65	£13.05
40	15	£24.95	£22.20
50	15	£54.40	£43.70
30	25	£14.15	£14.70
40	25	£30.60	£26.30

Example (b)
Smokers. Sum assured: £50,000

Age next birthday	Length of term (years)	Males	Females
30	10	£15.10	£18.55
40	10	£36.55	£32.95
50	10	£85.10	£68.20
30	15	£16.95	£19.65
40	15	£41.65	£36.50
50	15	£95.35	£75.15
30	25	£21.60	£22.70
40	25	£50.90	£43.30

Example (c)
Joint life cover. Sum assured: £50,000

Age next birthday	Term (years)	Non-smoker (both)	Smoker (both)
30	10	£18.60	£28.65
40	10	£37.65	£64.50
50	10	£83.45	£148.30
30	15	£19.70	£31.60
40	15	£42.15	£73.15
50	15	£93.10	£165.50
30	25	£23.86	£39.30
40	25	£51.90	£89.20

* When quoting for joint life cover, companies will use the age of the oldest partner in their calculations.

9 ║ *Other Types of Insurance*

Travel Insurance

The world is getting smaller. A generation ago most people went to the seaside for their holidays – and the seaside meant Blackpool, Clacton or Skegness. But thanks to dramatic reductions in the cost of air travel, millions of us now go abroad, sometimes several times a year. And we no longer simply want sun, sea and sand: we now head for exotic destinations in Asia and Africa. Long-distance flights to the American West Coast, Australia and New Zealand have brought relatives within easy reach. Each winter skiers flock in their tens of thousands to the European resorts and the Channel Tunnel has made the Continent more accessible for British travellers.

All this means that more of us are buying more travel insurance – with good reason, for this sort of cover is essential: the cost of falling ill while overseas can be frighteningly high. Most policies are sold alongside the holiday deal itself by the travel agent or tour operator, but cover is also available through insurance brokers. Shop around to get the best deal; don't simply accept whatever is offered when you book your trip. If you have a credit card, travel insurance may be an automatic benefit (offered by card providers in a bid to attract custom). Check with your card-provider to make sure you are not duplicating your cover needlessly.

Annual policies
Choice of policy has been further extended by the introduction of annual insurance policies aimed at people who travel abroad more than once a year. They provide cover automatically, wherever you

go. Originally developed for regular business travellers they are now becoming more widely available to reflect modern behaviour.

Annual policies usually offer big savings to frequent travellers. For example, a family with two children might pay £140 with this sort of contract for the full year's protection, compared with £150 for just two weeks' cover for a trip to the United States. However, there will usually be a time limit on the length of any one trip of 30, 60 or 90 days, so the policy would not be suitable for those travelling around the world, or for those who spend several months abroad at a time – elderly people wintering in Spain, for example.

Winter sports may be excluded, too. If you enjoy a summer holiday and a skiing trip, an annual policy might seem a good idea, but you will probably have to pay extra to extend the cover to winter sports. You may even find that it is not possible to extend the cover and you will be forced to buy a separate policy anyway.

What is covered by travel insurance?
A whole range of covers are included in standard travel insurance policies, reflecting the many things that can go wrong when you are travelling abroad. Basically, you are protecting yourself (and fellow-travellers for whom you are responsible), your belongings and the travel arrangements themselves.

If you are driving in Europe in your own car, you can extend the cover provided by your motor insurance policy by asking your broker or company for a Green Card. If you take your car further afield you may need to extend your cover with an additional premium, or buy a separate policy. If you hire a car while you are abroad, make sure that insurance is arranged when you pick up your vehicle. Don't skimp on cover to save a few pounds – the consequences could be financially catastrophic, especially in North America.

You might also consider breakdown insurance, which can be a huge help if you run into problems while touring. These policies will put you in touch with local garages, so you won't be hindered by communication problems. You can either buy them separately through your broker or insurance company or from one of the motoring organizations such as the AA or the RAC. Top-of-the-range motor insurance policies may also offer cover, perhaps for the payment of an extra premium. In any case, check your existing policy to make sure you don't go out and buy cover that you already have elsewhere.

Medical expenses
Under this section of your policy you will be covered for:

- **The cost of emergency treatment**, including hospital and associated medical bills. This will usually include emergency dental treatment. You may also be able to claim a cash amount for each day spent in hospital.
- **The cost of flying you back to the UK** in an air ambulance (known as repatriation) if this is deemed in your best interests. For example, you might receive emergency treatment abroad but want to recuperate at home. The insurer will also calculate the cost of flying you back to a British hospital and balance that against the cost of your treatment overseas. Your policy should provide for at least one person to accompany you on your flight (other than the necessary medical staff).
- **Any hotel or travel expenses** that result from injury or illness. This will include the extra costs associated with cutting your holiday short because of the medical problem. If you have to return home unexpectedly following the death of a relative, friend or business partner in the UK, your policy should reimburse any costs you incur.
- **The cost of burial or cremation abroad** or the cost of returning the body or ashes home to the UK.

There will be a limit on the amount that can be claimed under this section of the policy – £1m, £2m and £5m are common amounts.

As with normal medical insurance, it is absolutely vital that you tell the insurance company (on the proposal form) about any existing conditions from which you suffer. The same goes for any condition that might recur while you are away. You will still be able to get cover for emergencies, but the cost of continuing or routine treatment will not normally be met. You certainly won't be able to claim if you travel against medical advice.

Some people think that medical cover is unnecessary if they are travelling within the EC because of the reciprocal arrangements between the UK and other states, and this prompts them to try to manage without any insurance at all. This would be a mistake for two reasons: firstly, travel policies offer a lot more cover than protection against medical costs; and secondly, many costs fall outside the scope of the reciprocal agreements – not least the repatriation costs you might incur. Moreover, you would receive no contribution towards the cost of extra accommodation and travel for your family or anyone else who wanted to stay with you while you were in hospital.

Standards of State medical care vary widely in different European countries. In some places, private provision, as paid for by your travel insurance, might be the best (or even the only) way to obtain treatment equivalent to that offered in the UK.

Having said all that, the reciprocal arrangements can be useful, not least because many insurers will not charge an excess – the portion of the claim that you have to pay yourself – if you obtain basic treatment from the State. Form E111 (available from the Post Office) proves that you are from the UK and therefore entitled to treatment while in the EC.

If you do receive treatment or buy drugs on prescription while you are overseas, you *must* keep all the bills and receipts to help smooth the claims procedure.

Most insurance companies will provide an emergency telephone helpline number. Obviously, you will not always have time to contact the company before you are treated, but if possible you should call and seek advice first. The insurer's local contacts may be able to help you along. Take your policy documents with you – they should give you instructions on what to do in the event of a problem. At the very least, jot down a contact telephone number. Carrying that one piece of paper could save a lot of aggravation.

Personal accident

Personal accident cover pays a lump sum in the event of accidental death, the loss of a limb or sight, or following permanent total disablement during the holiday (or the travelling to or from your destination). Cover of up to £50,000 can be obtained in this section of the policy. Policies may also pay a weekly benefit – for example, £50 – in the case of temporary total disablement. Payment would continue while you were unable to work and cease when you started again.

Certain activities, such as scuba diving, parascending or motor-sports will be excluded by standard policies. Check your policy to see if any potentially hazardous holiday pursuits are specifically barred by your contract. You may be able to extend the scope of the cover with an extra premium.

If you are actually on holiday and want to do something for which you are not insured, think very carefully before going ahead. You may be able to buy cover on the spot if you are participating in an organized activity; otherwise, telephone the insurance company and ask for their advice.

If you regularly take part in a particular activity, such as pot-holding or climbing, you might be able to get a good deal through a club or national association – they can often negotiate favourable terms with insurance companies on behalf of their members.

Personal belongings

Your policy will also protect what you take with you on holiday, including clothes, cameras, personal stereos and cash. There will be a limit on the total amount you can claim – usually between £1,000 and £2,000, depending on the policy – and also on the amount that can be claimed on each particular item – £250, or perhaps £500. There will also be a similar limit on the amount of cash that can be insured.

Some policies will pay for your extra accommodation if you are unable to return home at the scheduled time because you have lost your passport and are waiting for a replacement. Any loss must be reported to the local police. Remember to ask them for proof of notification: your insurance company will certainly demand evidence that the loss was reported.

Insurance companies have paid out vast amounts for claims under this section of travel insurance policies and complain that many claims are fraudulent. You may find yourself tempted to try to take advantage of insurers by claiming for items that were not in fact lost. You would certainly not be unusual: after all, if every claim paid out for lost watches and cameras were genuine, it would not be possible to set foot on a beach in the Mediterranean without crunching a Rolex or a Pentax under foot. Remember, though, that policies carry an excess of £25 or £50 to discourage false claims and claims for items of little value. More importantly, falsifying an insurance claim is a criminal offence. Insurers are getting tough on fraud, so there is only one worthwhile piece of advice: don't do it.

If you have 'all-risks' cover on your household policy, valuable items may be insured already, although such duplication does not mean that you can claim for the same loss under two different policies! In some cases the travel insurance company will require you to claim for certain items under your household policy, which might invalidate any no claims bonus you have built up.

Travel policies require you to take reasonable care of your belongings and will not pay out if it can be proved that you were in any way negligent or reckless. To make sure you escape any such charge:

- Don't rely on huge amounts of cash. Buy travellers' cheques.
- Never leave belongings unattended.
- Use hotel safes if they are available.

- Follow advice from the authorities about where not to go. If you're the sort of person who instinctively wants to go to 'no-go' areas, at least try not to go alone.

Cancellation and curtailment

If you have to cancel your holiday or cut it short because of unforeseen circumstances, your policy should reimburse the cost of the trip. The accepted reasons for cancellation or curtailment may vary, but almost all policies recognize death, illness, injury, redundancy and jury service. Some policies will also accept that you may need to cancel or come home early following a burglary or fire at home, or a crisis at work. Different companies also have different ideas on who is included within this section: your policy may ask you to specify certain individuals or it may limit cover to close members of your family.

Remember that the policy will only serve to reimburse the cost of the holiday; it will not compensate for your disappointment with a cash payment. Neither will you be able to claim for the cost of clothes or other items that you bought in anticipation of the holiday.

Policies will not pay out if the holiday is cancelled or curtailed because of problems with the accommodation or other arrangements: these are the responsibility of the organizer, who is expected to reimburse you. You may be covered, however, if the organizer goes out of business and your holiday is cancelled as a result.

Delay

If your departure is delayed because of problems with the aircraft, train or sea vessel on which you are booked, or because of bad weather or strikes, you may receive a cash payment – say, £20 – for each hour of delay. There will be a waiting period of perhaps 12 hours, for which no payment will be made.

You may also be entitled to a cash payment if your baggage goes astray during the outward leg of the journey and there is a subsequent delay in getting it to you. Again, this will be calculated as an amount per hour elapsed following a certain waiting period. In both instances there will be a maximum pay-out of, perhaps, £1,000.

Missed departure

If you miss your flight, train or ferry departure, you may be able to claim a certain amount of compensation. The acceptable causes are usually interruptions to public transport or mechanical problems with your car. Claims for being stuck in a traffic jam are likely to be unsuccessful since the insurance company would argue that you should have left more time for the journey.

Liability and legal expenses

If you cause injury to a third party or damage a third party's property and incur a legal liability as a result, your policy will pay any claim that is awarded against you up to a pre-set limit of £1m or £5m, depending on the policy. This section will also pay any legal expenses associated with your defence. Your policy may also offer legal expenses insurance in its own right. This is intended to pay any costs incurred as you pursue someone else for damages following personal injury or death. The limit here is usually set at £25,000 or £50,000.

If you are injured or injure someone else during an activity that is specifically excluded by your policy, you may not be able to claim under this section of the policy.

Pet Insurance

Just as medical science has vastly improved the general level of health and life expectancy among humans, so advances in veterinary techniques have helped pets such as dogs, cats and horses to live happier, longer lives. But visiting the vet can be an expensive business. This has prompted the development of pet insurance, a policy designed to take care of medical fees and also provide for a range of other potential costs.

Pet insurance is available through insurance brokers but you are more likely to find cover through a vet or direct from the insurance company. Many advertise in magazines aimed at pet-owners. Vets are keen on insurance because it allows them to treat the animal according to its needs rather than according to the ability (or willingness) of the owner to foot the bill.

You can expect to pay between £50 and £70 a year for a cat and between £90 and £120 for a dog. Cover for other animals, such as rodents and birds, is less common – and you are highly unlikely to find cover for your fish (unless it is an extremely expensive ornamental breed such as Koi carp, which can be valued at many thousands of pounds and would therefore be insured against theft rather than vet's bills).

If you keep a horse or pony, you will need a specialist equine policy. Here the cost will be determined by the value of the beast. The policy, bought through a broker or through an advert in one of the horse magazines, might extend cover to the tack and other equipment – even the horse-box. You would certainly get liability cover, which is absolutely essential if you take your horse onto the public highway.

Whatever the animal, it will probably have to fall within a certain age range – the actual ages depend on the type and breed: a dog, for example, might have to be over 10 weeks and younger than 10 years. You will not be covered for any ailments which already afflicted the animal before you took out insurance.

Pet policies usually carry an excess, which means you contribute towards the cost of the claim. This will either be a fixed amount (£50 or £100) or will be calculated as a percentage (15%) of the claim.

What is covered?
Policies offer different covers and will pay up to certain limits within each category. You can determine the extent of your cover by the amount of premium you are willing to pay.

Veterinary fees: Bills will be met for illnesses and accident. However, policies will not cover the cost of vaccinations or of neutering or spaying; nor are they likely to reimburse you for any costs arising out of your pet's pregnancy. In other words, the policy will not pay out for voluntary expenditure or for situations that might have been avoided.

Third party liability: This covers you if your pet causes an accident that results in injury or damage and you are found to be legally liable.

Death: Policies will usually pay a death benefit up to the purchase price of the animal if it dies from an illness or accident. Death from old age does not trigger a payment.

Boarding fees: If you have to go into hospital, your policy might pay for separate accommodation for your animal while you are away. If you would rather leave the pet with a friend, the policy might pay a certain amount for each night you are indisposed.

Advertising and reward: If your animal is lost or stolen, your policy should contribute towards the cost of advertising for its return in the local newspaper and for the payment of an appropriate reward to the person who finds it. Horse- or pony-owners may be reimbursed for the costs of fetching a stolen animal home.

Loss by theft or straying: If the animal is lost, the policy will refund the purchase price. The required length of time before the animal is certified as lost varies. In cases where a claim is paid and the animal is subsequently discovered, you may be required to pay the money back.

Holiday cancellation: If you are forced to cancel your holiday because your pet needs urgent treatment and you want to stay with it, the pet policy would reimburse the cost of the holiday. This cover would not be available from a travel insurance policy.

Accidental damage: This covers any damage caused by your pet, either to your own property or to that of someone else. This cover is important if your house contents policy does not offer such protection.

Legal Expenses Insurance

Legal expenses insurance, which covers the cost of taking legal action, comes in two main forms: either as a 'stand-alone' policy, or as an 'add-on' to another insurance contract, usually a motor or household contents policy. Some of these policies include free legal expenses cover, but where this is the case allowable claims will be quite limited in scope.

Whichever form of protection you buy, the insurance covers legal expenses arising from litigation, such as the defence or pursuit of one's rights through civil action. Voluntary legal expenses – those normally involved in buying a house or drawing up a will, for example – are not covered. Nor will you be able to claim for the expenses associated with an existing problem which you know about before you took out the policy. It is always important to keep the insurance company fully informed of any matter that might result in a claim: most policies will only pay legal costs that are authorized by the insurer in advance. If, following an action in which your costs have been met by your policy, you are fined, your policy will not pay the cost of the fine itself.

Motorists' legal expenses cover

Motorists' legal expenses cover is sometimes known as 'uninsured loss recovery', or simply ULR. It normally costs less than £10 on top of a normal motor insurance premium and will relate to named individuals and a specific car.

The policy covers the cost of pursuing claims against other people for the repayment of uninsured losses arising from an accident. For example, if you have to hire another car following an accident that was not your fault, you might try to obtain payment from the guilty party. You might also use the legal expenses policy to prove that the other person was at fault in order to preserve your no claims bonus and avoid paying any excess when you get your car repaired.

Your policy may also offer free legal advice (which can often resolve a dispute without recourse to further action). With a top-drawer policy you may also get access to an accident and breakdown recovery service and free car-hire if yours is off the road; in addition it may cover you when you go abroad (although international cover is likely to be valid for only 30 days each year).

Householders' legal expenses cover

This type of cover can be added to a house contents policy to provide protection in a wide variety of cases. The most extensive (and expensive) contents policies may include legal expenses protection as standard. Your policy will cover your legal costs if, for example, you get into a dispute with a retailer or a manufacturer over the purchase of goods or services, or if you are at odds with your neighbours – perhaps over a right of way on your property or over the building of an extension which blocks the light. A legal helpline may also be available, where qualified staff offer advice on appropriate courses of action.

Stand-alone legal expenses cover

This is a catch-all policy that includes all the legal expenses cover offered in motorists' and householders' versions. In addition, it may fund costs associated with:

- Claims against other people for personal injury damages
- Disputes with your employer over your contract of employment
- Disputes with the Inland Revenue over personal taxation assessments
- Disputes over inheritance.

The free legal advice which is often included can be very valuable in helping you to decide whether or not you have a valid case.

All policies will set a limit – usually £50,000 on the amount that will be forthcoming for each claim. There will also be an aggregate limit on the amount that may be spent on all claims in any one year. The claims payment will cover solicitor's fees and expenses, the cost of barristers and expert witnesses, court costs and opponent's costs if these are awarded against you.

Boat insurance

Maintaining a boat without decent cover is no longer a sensible option. Craft themselves can be extremely expensive and modern vessels are often crammed with costly hi-tech navigational equipment. Satellite tracking systems, in particular, are readily portable and, in recent years, have become a prime target for theft. Theft from boats tends to occur when they are stored in yards for protracted periods or left unattended in marinas. Unlike car manufacturers, boat-builders don't usually have security at the forefront of their minds, so most boats do not present much of a challenge to thieves.

Insurance companies often require policyholders to keep a record of serial numbers of valuable items so that, if a stolen item is sent to the manufacturer for repair, they can track it down. However, they will always emphasize that your security should prevent the theft in the first place, and discounts may be available if security measures are implemented: small boats may have to be kept in a locked building; a trailer carrying a larger vessel should be fitted with wheel-clamps.

If your boat is moored in a marina, your discount will depend on the marina's level of security. Some sites challenge every visitor while others are very lax; it is clearly worth quizzing a marina about its attitude to this problem. Even the most secure complex can be vulnerable, however, so you yourself must always be vigilant.

Claims following material damage are also common. With smaller craft, such as racing dinghies, masts and sails are at risk; larger vessels tend to suffer underwater damage from running aground.

Policies also provide liability cover so that if you cause an accident at sea or something happens to a member of your crew, at least your legal costs will be indemnified.

The cost of insurance depends on the type of craft and its value; the annual premium will be roughly 1% of the value, so a £75,000 cruiser would attract a premium of between £700 and £800 while a £30,000 Westerley sailing yacht would be nearer to £300. A powerful speedboat worth £12,000, however, would cost around £500 to insure because of the higher potential risks. You may be able to obtain a no claims discount on your policy to help cut the cost of insurance in the future.

If you sail out of UK territorial waters, check the scope of your cover. Some policies only provide protection in certain areas and then only for a certain number of days per year.

Contingency Insurance

A range of policies is available under the general heading of contingency insurance. The word itself simply means a possible future event, so you are simply insuring yourself against an occurrence that would entail a loss or unwanted additional expenditure on your past. Clearly, most of the policies discussed in this book anticipate contingencies of one sort or another, but the most common ones, such as motor and household insurance, have developed descriptions of their own.

Special events

The organizers of an outdoor event might want to protect themselves against the possibility of a downpour, which would keep the crowds away and reduce their takings. The insurance – sometimes known as 'pluvius' cover – would also pay out if bad weather prevented the show from going ahead at all. The cost varies according to the location of the event, the time of the year, and the amount of money at stake.

This type of 'special events' cover provides other sorts of protection for those organizing events such as fêtes, sports days and outdoor concerts. For example, the organizer has certain potential liabilities with regard to the safety and security of those who pay to attend the event. There can also be difficulties if you provide car-parking (your 'Throw the Wellington' competitors may prove less than accurate). The policy will cover you for any claims for damage, injury or death and pay your associated legal costs.

Policies also include sections relating to any celebrity booked to open a show. Known as the 'death and disgrace' cover, this compensates you if your chosen star fails to shine on the day – whether due to death or injury or a tarnished reputation following a media exposé. In this last instance the celebrity might still want to come and pick up the fee, but if the nature of the misdemeanour means that you no longer feel that taking tea with the vicar and starting the children's races would be appropriate, you should be able to refuse this and to file your claim.

Special events cover can also protect you against the normal risks of damage to your equipment and theft of any takings, both at the show and (since many such events are held at the weekend) until the next banking day.

This insurance can also help you expand the scope of your show by allowing you to mount a money-spinning competition without incurring too much expense. For example, if you offer a car as a prize in a 'Roll-the-Dice' competition, you will attract a lot more interest than if the prize is a bottle of hooch or a dinner for two. The insurance simply means that if someone does manage to roll six sixes, the policy will pay for the car. (By the way, the odds of rolling six sixes in one go are 1 in 46,000. But for the sake of a few pounds in premium, is it a risk you are prepared to take?) Golf clubs often insure themselves against someone scoring a hole in one on the open day and winning the prize.

Wedding insurance

It sounds like a cracking idea: an insurance policy that pays out if married life turns out to be less fulfilling and enjoyable than you thought it would be. Alas, the industry has yet to come up with such a contract. The weddings insurance policies on offer insure the event itself against cancellation due to circumstances beyond the control of those involved. In other words the policy will not pay if the bride or groom simply fail to show up. Acceptable grounds for a claim are illness, injury or delay due to unavoidable problems: you might have a temperamental vintage car or pony and trap, for instance. You can also insure any clothing you hire for the big day, and rings and presents can be covered for loss, theft or damage. If, for some reason, the wedding photos don't come out, you can receive a lump sum to pay for the cost of re-staging the event in order to get an albumful of decent shots.

The cost of the insurance is determined by the amount of cover you require: wedding magazines estimate the average cost of a full-blown event to be anywhere between £8,000 and £15,000. You should expect to pay at least £40 for a basic policy and up to £100 at the upper end of the scale.

Twins

If you are trying to conceive, you can insure yourself against the risk of a multiple birth. The cost of more than one child arriving at once can cause problems, so the insurance will take care of reasonable costs above and beyond what you might reasonably expect to spend on one baby.

Funeral plans

Some people think of it as the ultimate in financial planning: an insurance policy that pays for your funeral. These plans are increasing in popularity: a typical funeral costs £1,100, so elderly people like to know that they are not going to leave their families with this financial burden when they finally go the way of all flesh.

If you opt to 'pre-pay' the cost of your funeral, you are effectively buying the funeral service you want at today's prices, either by lodging a lump sum with the insurance company or by making regular monthly payments for the rest of your life. You can therefore stipulate the sort of funeral you want, and pay accordingly.

There are a number of points to watch out for when making your arrangements: Does the policy guarantee to pay all the costs associated with burial? Will the cover be valid if you move and die in a different area of the country? Does the policy leave your family with a choice of undertaker or oblige them to use a certain firm? Whatever the answers to these questions, make sure your heirs and any trustees you appoint to look after your estate are fully aware of your plans.

Unusual Risks

As already mentioned at the beginning of this book, you can insure almost anything. All you have to do is present a certain amount of information to an insurance underwriter and pay whatever premium is deemed appropriate for the risks involved. Footballers insure their legs, singers insure their voices, pianists insure their fingers, models insure their assets.

Lloyd's of London
Risks of this nature are usually insured at Lloyd's of London. This is not an insurance company in the accepted sense; it is a market where brokers approach organizations called syndicates, which tend to specialize in certain types of insurance. There are several hundred syndicates covering everything from satellites to submarines. If a particularly big risk is involved, the broker will distribute the premium among a number of syndicates in order to spread the potential pay-out.

Lloyd's brokers often have close relationships with regional broking firms, so you can find your way into the Lloyd's market through your local broker. Some Lloyd's brokers dealing with motor insurance have started advertising direct to the public. It is not possible to deal direct with a Lloyd's syndicate.

Lloyd's has been in the news recently because many of the individuals (the 'Names') whose money pays the claims have been bankrupted by huge losses, mainly arising from incidents like hurricanes in North America, the Piper Alpha oil rig catastrophe, and compensation claims from those who have contracted industrial diseases such as asbestosis. However, these Names are alleging that a mixture of incompetence and skulduggery on the part of those responsible for managing their affairs has turned a bad situation into a disaster. Various court cases, inquiries and investigations will be required to decide whether the Names – whose entire personal assets may be at stake – have been fairly treated and how they should be compensated.

This messy situation might give Lloyd's policyholders some cause for concern, especially if they have bought vital motor or household insurance through the market. However, Lloyd's has never defaulted on a claim and the market's governing authorities have their own contingency reserves that can be called upon if necessary to make sure that policyholders receive their due. It is also worth pointing out that, while many syndicates at Lloyd's have undoubtedly suffered substantial losses, others – especially those dealing in the mainstream insurance products available to the general public – have continued to be profitable.

10 | *Sorting Out Your Insurance Needs*

Deep down, we all know we need insurance, but it is the last thing we want to spend our money on. Insurance is there in case something bad happens, so when you pay your premium, you are acknowledging that you might crash your car, that your house might be burgled, that you might lose your job, fall ill or die – none of them pleasant prospects, which is why we don't spend money on insurance policies with the same enthusiasm as we buy new clothes or a video recorder.

If we are reluctant to buy insurance, it follows that we want the best possible value for money. We don't want policies we don't need, and we definitely don't want to pay over the odds for essential protection. So don't rush your insurance purchases just to get the unpleasant business out of the way as soon as possible; assess your needs coolly and responsibly, decide what you need and then hunt around for the best deal.

This sort of approach takes longer, but it means that you can be confident that you have the protection you require, and that you are not spending money on insurance that could be put to good use elsewhere in your budget. Remember that a salesman will advise you to spend every penny of free cash on insurance; it is up to you to be realistic and identify your priorities.

Where to Start

Once you have decided to bite the bullet and get your insurance affairs in order, you need to get the trusty pen and paper out and, under a big heading called 'Protection', actually jot down what cover you have, what it costs you, where the gaps are and how much they would cost to fill. Here are some basic sub-headings that apply to virtually everyone; they should give some structure to your thoughts.

Me and my family

Under this heading, think about your financial well-being. Ask yourself the tough questions: what would happen if I died? How would those who depend on me survive? If you have a partner and, perhaps, children, think about the consequences of their deaths as well. What would happen to the family income? Just as importantly, what would happen to expenditure? Would there be sudden extra demands that would make a bad situation even worse?

Death is not the only possibility; other catastrophes could also play havoc with your financial well-being. What if you or your partner couldn't work because of an accident or because you fell seriously ill? Do you have insurance protection for your outstanding debts so that they would be settled or at least serviced if you were no longer earning a regular income? Have you any resources that would help you to survive a downturn in your personal fortune, or do you need to plan for possible problems in advance?

My possessions

If you drive a car, you need to buy insurance (unless, of course, it is already provided by your employer). But what sort of cover do you need: an expensive top-of-the-range policy with a host of extras attached, or a basic contract that satisfies the legal obligations?

You need insurance on your house and the belongings it contains. But again, do you want to pay for the bells and whistles attaching to the most expensive contracts, or are you happy with a more standard offering? Do you own anything of high value, such as a collection, jewellery or antiques, that might need a separate policy?

Cars and houses obviously need to be covered, but you may have other possessions that could also benefit from insurance protection. Do you have any pets? Do you own a boat or a caravan? Try to build a picture of your family situation and think about the benefits of having insurance.

Occasional needs

You should also be prepared to spend some money on a more occasional basis. For example, you should make sure you have travel insurance each time you go abroad. And if you are ever involved in organizing a special event, be it a village fête or a wedding, you might want to arrange suitable insurance. In other words, you should try to include insurance within your general budgeting, so that it is not always at the bottom of your list and either ignored or bought in a hurry.

Once you have a broad idea of what insurance cover you should buy, you can refer to the chapter headings in this book to see more precisely where you are at present and where you would like to be.

Buying insurance

Choosing good cover at the right price takes time and effort. Companies competing for business are constantly bombarding us with advertisements, and the wide selection of policies can be confusing. But this competition at least puts you, the customer, in the driving seat: companies will be only too happy to supply you with all the information you need, so play the field, and don't take the first offer you see. The time you spend shopping around may save you a great deal of money.

Brokers

The job of a broker is to do your shopping around for you but, as you might expect, some brokers are better than others. What is more, brokers will not obtain quotes for you from companies that only sell direct to the public (since these companies will not pay commission), so they will not necessarily find you the best policy at the best price. Unless you know a broker whom you trust to act in your interests, why not consult a number of brokers *and* companies that sell direct before making your decision?

Each insurance company and broker spends a lot of money trying to persuade you that it offers the best policy, but of course they can't all be right. If a company claims that you can save £££s by its policies, by all means give it a hearing – very often one company *will* be £££s cheaper than another – but never take what you are told on trust.

Insurance in real life situations

You can often get a clearer picture of your own needs by looking at someone else's situation. Clearly, no two cases will be alike in every detail, but seeing how other people approach the subject, tackle the problems and make the most of the opportunities can be enlightening.

In the following cases, not every aspect of the individuals' insurance requirements is discussed: we can assume that they have followed the golden rule of shopping around for good value protection and have not encountered any major problems. Only issues of specific interest have been highlighted.

Case A	Mary Slater
Age	22
Status	Single
Dependants	None
Occupation	Junior accountant
Salary	£12,000
Home	Rented flat, Didsbury, South Manchester

Mary is in her first year of full-time work after finishing her degree. She is paying off her student loan and still has an overdraft from her college days, so money is tight, but she is beginning to think more seriously about insurance and financial products in general, and knows that she should be making some provision for the unexpected.

As she has no dependants and no major capital debts, she doesn't really need any life insurance. Indeed, she told the salesman who tried to persuade her to take out a policy that she simply could not think who she would want the money to go to.

Living in rented accommodation, Mary does not have to worry about buildings insurance, but she does need protection for her contents. She reckons these are worth between £7,000 and £8,000 but finds that many insurers impose a minimum sum insured of £10,000 on their contents policies, so she asks her broker for a contract that caters for her requirements. He finds a stripped-down contract offering basic insurance protection with the correct sum insured which is £40 cheaper than the cheapest mainstream policy.

Mary was given a new Golf GTi (already insured!) by her parents as a graduation present and is worried about the cost of paying for cover when it comes to renewal. She has been told by friends that younger drivers of sporty cars often pay significantly higher premiums than drivers over 25 with typical family saloons. However, by shopping around she finds a 'women only' policy providing fully comprehensive cover and excellent post-accident and breakdown assistance services for 25% less than her parents paid.

As far as medical insurance is concerned, Mary is content to wait until she has been with her present employer for two years, when she becomes eligible for the company scheme. She has a hankering for income replacement insurance, but accepts that she cannot yet afford it.

Case B	Tim Jeffries
Age	31
Status	Married
Dependants	Emma (4), Ben (2)
Occupation	Production controller
Salary	£14,000, plus variable overtime

Spouse	Karen Jeffries
Occupation	Housewife and mother
Home	Owner of terraced house, Partick, Glasgow

Tim's main concern is Karen and the children: what would happen to them if he were to be killed. His father died in a car crash when Tim was in his teens and he remembers how his mother struggled to bring him and his brothers up on the small pension provided by his father's firm. He is therefore determined that Karen will not be put in a similar situation, especially as he is not in a company pension scheme.

When Tim is visited at home by an insurance salesman, he asks for details of what the firm has to offer and is given a quote for 20-year term cover of £60,000 for both him and Karen which will pay out when the first one of them dies. However, he decides to double-check with a local broker, who says that the company's quote of £24 per month is expensive and comes up with an alternative at under £19.

Initially, Tim is worried, since he suspects the cheaper policy may in some way be inferior, but he is reassured when the broker tells him that term assurance really is a case of 'What you see is what you get'. In other words, as long as the insurance company is financially strong enough to honour its obligations (which it is), there is nothing to be gained by paying any more for the same amount of protection.

The £60,000 figure surprised Tim, who thought it might be high, but he eventually agreed that the salesman's figures were accurate: it would cost him a significant amount to pay for help in the home and looking after the children if Karen were killed. Indeed, the salesman wanted to push him higher, but with an eye on the size of the premium, Tim calculated that in the event of a tragedy he would get a certain amount of help – with baby-sitting, if nothing else – from grandparents.

Tim's other big worry is the mortgage. His endowment

policy should ensure it is paid off at maturity if he continues to pay the premiums and it will certainly clear the debt if either he or Karen is killed, but he is concerned about job security and wonders what will happen if he is made redundant or cannot work for any other reason. His building society suggests a mortgage payment protection policy, which costs £18 per month and provides £300 of benefit per month towards his interest payments and associated insurance premiums.

Case C	**Martin Coombs**
Age	46
Status	Married
Dependants	Nick (16), Sarah-Louise (12)
Occupation	Civil engineer
Salary	£40,000, plus £2,000 bonus
Spouse	Elizabeth Tompkinson
Occupation	Freelance interior designer
Salary	Variable
Home	Detached house, Cheltenham

Martin Coombs has reached that difficult age when most men realize that they are not immortal after all: Nick, his son, has beaten him at squash for the first time ever. Waking up the next morning with aching limbs and a heavy heart, he acknowledges his true situation and resolves to get his financial affairs in good order so that his family is protected – and to start going to a gym.

Martin already has in place a family income policy which will pay an income for a set number of years if either he or Elizabeth dies; he is also in a company pension scheme which will pay a lump sum of four times his salary to Elizabeth in addition to a widow's pension. However, in his new reflective mood he wants protection in case he has to stop work because of illness.

When he discusses the issue of income replacement with his broker, he finds out how precarious his position has been to date: he would receive less than £75 a week from the State once his six-month entitlement to Statutory Sick Pay had elapsed. With two children at private school, this would obviously not go very far, but at least he arranged mortgage protection insurance when the family moved to its present home two years ago; this would at least ensure that the major financial commitment was taken care of each month.

Elizabeth had income protection insurance of her own. She had actually worked for a bank before taking a career break to have the children, and had been persuaded of the wisdom of having cover. When she became self-employed as the kids got older and her contribution to the family income became increasingly significant, she took out a policy again (she failed to persuade Martin because in those days he was still beating Nick at squash and couldn't see why a policy would ever be necessary).

Martin finally decides that a monthly benefit of £750 represents a realistic compromise between affordable premiums and his normal monthly take-home pay of just over £2,000. The policy, which is designed to pay out after a 13-week waiting period, costs between £63 and £110 per month depending on the insurance company, so he is pleased that he shopped around and didn't simply take the first policy he was offered.

During his investigations Martin also came across critical illness insurance, which pays out if certain conditions, such as cancer or heart disease, are diagnosed. However, protection worth £50,000 until he retires at 60 would cost him around £50 per month and he decides that this, on top of his income replacement premiums, is just too much. There are limits on a man's perceptions of his own frailty.

Case D	John Hopkins
Age	65
Status	Married
Dependants	None
Occupation	Retired works manager
Spouse	Sally Hopkins
Home	Semi-detached house, Bournemouth

John and Sally Hopkins have been looking forward to John's retirement (Sally has never gone to work). They will enjoy visiting friends and relatives, taking extended holidays and generally spending more time in each other's company. However, they realize that if their dream of a comfortable retirement is to become a reality, they need to husband their resources. John has a decent enough pension from his job: when added to their State entitlements it should enable them to live well enough, but they cannot be rash in their spending. This means checking to see that every penny spent on insurance is spent wisely.

Every year John shops around carefully when it comes time to renew the house and car insurance policies. He has used the same broker every year but always telephones a few of the companies that sell direct to double-check that he is not paying over the odds. Now that he is 65 he finds that many of the direct insurers propose to charge him more. On enquiry, he discovers that he no longer fits the 'target profile' of a middle-aged driver of a saloon. Luckily, his broker is able to find a company that takes his many years of safe driving into account and charges him a premium close to what he has been paying previously.

When it comes to home insurance, however, the broker has much better news: a number of companies are offering discounts to retired people on the basis that they tend to keep their homes in good order and are less susceptible to burglaries because they are more likely to be at home during the day. John tells the broker that he and Sally want to do a bit of travelling, but the broker reassures him that the only qualification for the discount is age; there is no requirement to promise to stay indoors all day. As a result, instead of paying £240 for £80,000 of buildings cover and £35,000 of contents cover, he gets his protection for less than £230.

While they are looking forward to the next few years of their lives, John and Sally are conscious that they are entering a stage in their lives when their health is increasingly likely to fail. After reading an article in a weekend newspaper about a policy called long term care cover, Sally finds out from her broker that it is the ideal time for her and John to insure themselves. They therefore arrange a policy that will pay out when both of them become unable to look after themselves properly at home (they assume that if one of them falls ill or becomes confused, the other will provide the necessary care).

The benefit level chosen is £500 per month (which will be linked to inflation). This will be used to pay for nursing care and accommodation as required. The joint policy costs a little over £80 per month; although this is a significant amount, they judge it to be worth paying because they are determined not to become a burden on their children, who have long since left home and started families of their own.

Conclusions

Someone once said of insurance that you never need it until you need it. What he meant was that you never find out whether your policy is any good until you actually make a claim – and then, of course, it is too late to do anything about it. So make sure that you buy wisely:

- Assess your needs properly
- Take your time to work out what you can afford

- Shop around
- Review your policies regularly.

You won't have much fun doing this, but you will earn yourself a good deal of satisfaction and peace of mind and possibly save yourself some money to boot.

11 ‖ *How to Complain*

Many insurance products are very complex and, as a buyer, you face a bewildering choice, not only of types of policy, but also of ways to buy your cover. For example, do you go to a broker for the benefit of impartial and expert advice, or do you trust your own judgement and buy direct from an insurance company in a bid to trim a few pounds off the premium?

It is extremely difficult to be categoric and to say that one option will always be better than another for everyone in every situation. So no matter how much reading around the subject you do, no matter how much advice you take, no matter how much you discuss matters with friends and relations, there will come a point where you are going to have to make your own decisions.

You will not, however, be completely on your own. The complexity of the insurance market has been acknowledged by the Government and by the industry itself and various independent complaints and arbitration mechanisms have been set up. These are designed to help insurance buyers if they get into a dispute, either with their broker or with the insurance company itself.

How to Complain to an Insurance Company or Broker

If you do want to pursue a grievance against any commercial organisation, always go first of all to that organization itself. Most companies have well-established complaints procedures and should be able to respond constructively to any matters you want to raise. They will certainly not want the issue to go to an outside body if at all possible, so they will probably give you a fair hearing.

If you bought your policy through a broker and subsequently

have a dispute with the insurance company, ask the broker to take on the case on your behalf. This sort of service is one of the things covered by your commission. Here are a list of steps you might take when complaining direct to the broker or insurance company:

1 When using the telephone, make a note of the time and date of each call and ask for the name of the person you are speaking to. Jot down the gist of your conversation, especially any statement concerning measures the company intends to take. You can be sure that the company will keep records of this sort, so you should do likewise. This will be a big help if the dispute drags on for any length of time.

2 If your first couple of phone calls produce no results, put your complaint in writing. Keep a copy of every letter you send (and every reply you receive, no matter how inconsequential it may seem). For the sake of clarity, it is better to type your letters than to write by hand. Use one side of the paper only in case a sheaf of papers is photocopied together and a side missed as a result.

3 Provide full details about yourself and your policy. Check your policy documents for reference numbers and policy numbers and include these at the head of your letter. This will speed up the process.

4 Lodge your initial enquiry or complaint with a local manager or with the person mentioned on your policy document. If you have bought direct from a company over the telephone, ask the company to whom you should write.

5 If you do not obtain satisfaction from your initial complaint or enquiry, tell that person that you intend to pursue the matter with his or her superiors. This may work wonders in getting things resolved.

6 Should you have to write to a managing director, chairman or chief executive, provide a brief summary of your

grievance but don't feel obliged to include every last detail. If the boss is worth his or her salt, the appropriate wheels will soon be set in motion and you should see some action.

7 If you still get no results, write again to the most senior person in the organization and tell him or her that you are going to seek outside assistance. Mention the specific body you propose to contact to show that you mean business: this might just be enough of a threat to settle matters to your satisfaction.

8 If you still find yourself getting nowhere with the company itself, take your problem to one of the bodies listed below. Include as much detail as you can, including copies of all the relevant correspondence. As you write, try to imagine you have no knowledge of your situation; think what information you would need to bring you up to date.

9 Be patient. Getting to the root of an insurance problem can take a long time, so be prepared to wait. However, make sure that you don't let your insurance lapse during the course of a dispute. This could happen with an annual policy, such as household insurance: you may not want to renew your cover with the company you have fallen out with, but do make alternative arrangements where necessary.

10 Try not to lose your temper! Shouting at people on the other end of the telephone rarely makes things better and can sometimes make things worse.

Getting Outside Help

The Insurance Ombudsman Bureau
According to *The Oxford English Dictionary*, 'ombudsman' is a word of Swedish origin meaning: 'An official appointed to investigate complaints by individuals against maladministration

by public authorities.' As the pro-consumer lobby has developed in recent years, Ombudsmen (and -women) have appeared in many different sectors, including the insurance and financial sectors.

As a general rule, you should contact an Ombudsman within six months of coming up against a brick wall in your negotiations with the insurance company.

Although membership of the Insurance Ombudsman Bureau is voluntary, most UK insurance companies are members. There are, however, one or two notable exceptions (such as the Co-operative Insurance Society and BUPA), and this has led to calls for a compulsory scheme of some kind.

The firms that belong to the bureau have accepted a rule which says that they must abide by any decision made by the Ombudsman. However, the IOB's rules also state that it is unable to consider a complaint until that complaint has been considered and rejected by the chief executive of the insurance company concerned. Complaints must then be lodged with the Ombudsman within six months of the final rejection by the company.

Complaints to the Ombudsman fall into three main categories:

- **Mis-selling**: This means whoever sold the policy made false statements to the policyholder about what was covered or about what the policy was intended to provide.
- **Ambiguity**: If the wording of the policy is construed to be ambiguous, the benefit of the doubt will normally be given to the policyholder.
- **Mistakes**: If the insurance company makes a mistake (normally during the claims process) that leads to the policyholder suffering a loss, an award may be made against the company.

Roughly 60% of the cases dealt with by the Ombudsman are found in favour of the insurance company. Something over 30% result in victories for the policyholder, with the remainder either being settled or dropped before a decision is reached. When the decision is in favour of the policyholder, the insurance company will either be required to pay compensation or to deal with the claim in accordance with the policy conditions as they have been interpreted by the Ombudsman.

There is also a Banking Ombudsman and a Building Societies Ombudsman, but these deal with the main business operations of the organizations involved. Most banks and building societies act as insurance agents on behalf of insurance companies, so if you have an insurance-related complaint against a bank or building society and get no joy from the institution's own complaints procedure, you will probably be referred to the company whose products it is selling. It is highly likely that this company will belong to the Insurance Ombudsman Bureau.

The Insurance Ombudsman Bureau
City Gate One
135 Park Street
London SE1 9EA
Tel: 0171 928 4488

The PIA Ombudsman
While the IOB deals with insurance policies that contain no investment element, the Personal Investment Authority Ombudsman is concerned with products that are regulated under the Financial Services Act, the central plank of regulation governing the investment industry in the UK. Remember that insurance and investment are not the same. The first pays out when (or if) a certain event occurs, while the second attempts to provide a return on a capital sum, either in the form of growth or in the provision of a regular income.

As far as this book is concerned, the only products that would fall within the ambit of the PIA ombudsman would be endowment and certain whole of life policies. If you have a problem in this regard and are not sure who to turn to for help, the adviser or company that supplied the product should be able to tell you which organization regulates their business. If the answer is the PIA, which it probably will be, at least you know where to go.

The Personal Investment Authority Ombudsman
1 London Wall
London EC2 5EA
Tel: 0171 600 4727

Other bodies
In addition to the Insurance and PIA Ombudsmen, there are various statutory bodies which may be able to help with your specific problem:

Personal Investment Authority
3–4 Royal Exchange Buildings
London EC3V 3NL
Tel: 0171 538 8860

Insurance Brokers Registration Council
15 St Helen's Place
London EC3A 6DS
Tel: 0171 588 4387

Investors' Compensation Scheme
Gavrelle House
2–14 Bunhill Row
London EC1Y 8RA
Tel: 0171 638 1240

Trade associations
Most insurance organizations belong to trade associations. These bodies often have internal disciplinary procedures that might help you; they will certainly be keen to maintain the good name of their members and should therefore at least investigate your problem if you are in dispute with a particular organization.

An organization's official stationery will normally provide details of any trade body to which it belongs.

Association of British Insurers
51 Gresham Street
London EC2V 7HQ
Tel: 0171 600 3333

British Insurance and Investment Brokers Association
14 Bevis Marks
London EC3A 7NT
Tel: 0171 623 9043

The Independent Financial Adviser Association
12–13 Henrietta Street
Covent Garden
London WC2E 8LH
Tel: 0171 240 7878

Independent Financial Adviser Promotion
28 Greville Street
London EC1N 8SU
Tel: 0117 971 1177

Institute of Insurance Brokers
Higham Business Centre
Midland Road
High Ferrers NN9 8DW
Tel: 01933 410003

Other useful addresses

Consumers' Association
2 Marylebone Road
London NW1 4DF
Tel: 0171 486 5544

Lloyd's of London
Lime Street
London EC3 7DG
Tel: 0171 623 7100

Royal Institution of Chartered Surveyors
12 Great George Street
Parliament Square
London SW1P 3AD

The Data Protection Registrar
The work of the Data Protection Registrar is to ensure that companies and other organizations do not misuse or abuse information concerning individuals that is held on computer. If you think a company has incorrect information about you, it is obliged to reveal that information and correct it where appropriate. There are also rules governing the sharing of information concerning individuals between organizations. However, businesses and other bodies are free to store information in the public domain, such as that found on the Electoral Roll.

If in doubt on any matter related to computer files containing details of yourself or members of your family, contact the Registrar:

The Data Protection Registrar
Wycliffe House
Water Lane
Wilmslow
Cheshire SK9 5AF
Tel: 01625 535777

APPENDIX I

The Leading Telephone-based Insurance Companies and Brokers

Company	Tel:
Admiral	0800 373355
AA Insurance Services	0800 444777
Churchill	0800 200300 (motor)
	0800 200345 (household)
Commercial Union	0800 230800
Cornhill Direct	0800 607070
Direct Line	Numbers vary; consult *Yellow Pages*
Eagle Star Direct	0800 770600 (motor)
	0800 770660 (household)
Frizzell	01202 292333
GA Direct	0800 121000 (motor)
	0800 121004 (household)
Guardian Direct	0800 282820
Insurance Service, The	0800 989898 (motor)
	0800 878787 (household)
Landmark Express	0500 555500
Preferred Direct	0800 850750
Premium Search	0800 109876
Privilege	Numbers vary; consult *Yellow Pages*
Prospero	0800 747576
Royal Direct	0500 223344
Telesure	0181 665 9988
Touchline	0800 207700

To obtain a list of insurance brokers, contact the British Insurance
& Investment Brokers Association (tel: 0171 623 9043).
  For a list of independent advisers, call IFA Promotion (tel: 0117
971 1177).

Companies in the Second-hand Endowment Market

Company	Tel:
Absolute Assigned Policies	0181 951 1996
Association of Policy Market Makers	0171 739 3949
Beale Dobie & Co.	01621 851133
H. E. Foster & Cranfield (Auctioneers)	0171 608 1941
Neville James Ltd	01730 233000
PolicyPlus International	01225 466466
Policy Portfolio	0181 343 4567
Securitised Endowment Contracts	0181 207 1666
Surrenda-Link	01244 317999

As you read through your insurance documentation you will probably come across some unfamiliar words. Listed below are the main insurance terms with brief explanations.

Actuary An insurance company employee whose job it is to assess risks and calculate appropriate premiums.

Agent A person who sells insurance on behalf of one or more companies.

All risks An optional extension on policies that provide cover for property. This wider range of cover most commonly protects items such as cameras outside the home.

Average The process whereby the amount paid out by the insurance company is reduced if the policyholder has not insured property to its full value. If the property is under-insured by 20%, for example, the claim payment will be reduced by the same percentage.

Benefit The money paid on a life insurance policy when a claim is made.

Bonus The amount added to the sum insured of a with profits life insurance policy, either during the term of the policy (the 'reversionary' bonus) or when the policy matures (the 'terminal' bonus).

Broker A person or business that is registered with the Insurance Brokers Registration Council. Brokers sell on behalf of a wide range of insurance companies and either earn commission or charge fees to their customers.

Buildings insurance Cover for the structure of your house.

Comprehensive insurance A policy (usually motor) that covers a number of different risks.

Conditions The rules within a policy that must be followed if claims are to be paid.

Contents insurance Cover for your possessions.

Cover note A document that provides evidence of cover while the actual policy certificate is being prepared.

Critical illness insurance A policy that pays a lump sum when one of a range of serious illnesses is diagnosed.

Deductible *see* Excess.

Direct insurance This is where policies are bought direct from the company, rather than through an agent or broker.

Endorsement An amendment to a policy that changes the scope and nature of the cover provided.

Endowment A policy that pays out a lump sum either at the end of a specified period or earlier if the policyholder dies.

Excess (or Deductible) The amount that must be paid by the policyholder towards the cost of the claim.

Exclusion A description of an item, person or event that is not covered by the policy.

Family income policy A policy that pays a regular benefit for a specified length of time to the surviving family of the insured person following that person's death.

Green card A document used by UK motorists driving their own cars overseas to prove that they have adequate insurance for each country visited.

Holiday insurance Protection against cancellation, delay, lost or stolen baggage and the cost of medical treatment while abroad.

Household insurance The collective term for buildings and contents insurance.

Income replacement cover A policy that pays benefits while the policyholder is unable to work because of illness or accident.

Indemnity terms The type of insurance that, following a loss, restores the policyholder to his or her previous financial position.

Index-linking The process of changing a sum insured or benefit in line with a recognized index, such as the Retail Price Index.

Introductory bonus A reduction in standard premiums charged by some motor insurers to new policyholders.

Legal expenses insurance A policy that covers the cost of legal proceedings.

Liability Legal responsibility for injuring another person or damaging his or her property.

Long-term care insurance A policy that pays nursing and accommodation costs when policyholders are no longer able to manage on their own.

Loss adjuster A person paid by an insurance company to check the validity of a claim and to negotiate the size of the claim.

Loss assessor A person paid by a policyholder to negotiate with the insurance company.

Maturity value The value of a policy when it reaches the end of its term.

Medical insurance Cover against the costs of private medical treatment.

Mortgage payment protection policy A policy that covers monthly mortgage payments and related outgoings in the event of sickness, accident or unemployment

New for old cover (also known as 'replacement' terms) Cover that replaces items with brand-new replacements. The alternative is to make a deduction for the wear and tear assumed to be suffered by older items.

No claims discount (or bonus) A reduction in premium awarded in recognition of an absence of claims over a given period.

Permanent health insurance *see* Income replacement insurance.

Personal accident insurance A policy that pays out when the policyholder is injured in an accident. The benefit may be paid weekly or monthly or as a lump sum.

Premium rate The price of the insurance. It may sometimes be expressed as an amount per unit of cover. An example would be house buildings insurance, where the cost is often quoted as 'pence per hundred', which means you pay, say, 25 pence for every £100 of cover you need. This would be written as £0.25 per £100 or 25p per cent.

Proposal form The application form for insurance cover.

Renewal notice An invitation from your present insurer to take out another policy when the existing one expires.

Sum insured The maximum amount the policy will pay out in the event of a claim. With an endowment policy, the sum insured is the amount the company guarantees to pay, either at maturity or earlier if a claim arises. This amount may be increased through the addition of bonuses.

Surrender value The amount paid to a policyholder if an endowment policy is discontinued before the end of the term.

Term insurance Life insurance that lasts for a specified time. If the policyholder survives until the end of the term, no benefit is paid.

Third party Another person involved in a claim made by the policyholder (the second party is the insurance company).

Underwriter The person or company who accepts the risk and charges the premium. Policies often state that the risk is 'underwritten' by the company concerned.

Unit-linked A type of investment where insurance premiums buy units in a fund and the value of the policy is subsequently 'linked' to the performance of the fund as a whole.

Whole of life policy A policy where premiums are paid throughout the policyholder's life, and where the benefit is paid whenever the policyholder dies.

With profits A type of investment where insurance premiums are invested in a variety of ways and any profits (minus deductions for expenses and, in some cases, shareholder dividends) are distributed to policyholders in the form of bonuses.

Write-off A damaged vehicle that is either beyond repair or is in such a bad state that it would cost more to repair than it was worth before the damage occurred. Also known as a 'total loss'.

INDEX

The Sunday Times
Personal Finance Guide to
Tax-free Savings
How to Make Your Money Work Hardest For You

Christopher Gilchrist

Are you making the most of your savings and investments?

Nobody enjoys paying tax but few people make full use of the many opportunities now available to everyone in the UK to save and invest tax-free. This guide explains the basics of tax and investment and shows how you can use tax-free plans to make more of your money, including:

- how moving your savings into tax-free schemes can boost your returns
- how to work out what you need to save for retirement and the best tax-exempt ways to do so
- the differences between lower-risk, moderate-risk and high-risk schemes and how much each could produce for you
- identifying the saving and investment plans that offer the best value for money
- the best plans for short-term and longer-term savings

Over a period of twenty years, £100 a month placed in a building society account might accumulate to £45,000. But a good tax-exempt savings plan linked to shares could turn that same £100 a month into £130,000.

Taking the right decisions now on where to save your surplus income could add tens of thousands of pounds to your personal wealth.

0 00 638703 9

HarperCollinsPaperbacks